AMC Cars

1954–1987

An Illustrated History

Patrick R. Foster

Iconografix

Iconografix
1830A Hanley Road
Hudson, Wisconsin 54016 USA

Library of Congress Control Number: 2003115056

ISBN-13: 978-1-58388-112-5
ISBN 1-58388-112-3

Reprinted January 2012

Printed in The United States of America

Copyedited by Suzie Helberg

Cover Photos:

Upper left: The 1954 Hudson marked the end of the great Detroit-built Hudsons, known as the step-down models.

Upper right: AMC Eagle was the first four-wheel-drive passenger car from an American producer, and the last model to wear the AMC badge. A 1982 model is shown.

Middle left: The Rambler American two-door sedan was part of the exceptionally popular and successful Rambler line for 1962.

Middle right: Javelin was AMC's entry into the pony car market and it proved to be an important image builder. Javelin also won fame in Trans-Am racing.

Lower left: AMC Hornet replaced the Rambler in 1970 and was billed as "The Little Rich Car". Shown is a 1972 model.

Lower right: One of the most controversial cars of all time, the uniquely styled Pacer hatchback was a very popular car when it was introduced in 1975.

BOOK PROPOSALS

Iconografix is a publishing company specializing in books for transportation enthusiasts. We publish in a number of different areas, including Automobiles, Auto Racing, Buses, Construction Equipment, Emergency Equipment, Farming Equipment, Railroads & Trucks. The Iconografix imprint is constantly growing and expanding into new subject areas.

Authors, editors, and knowledgeable enthusiasts in the field of transportation history are invited to contact the Editorial Department at Iconografix, Inc., 1830A Hanley Rd, Hudson, WI 54016

Dedication

I'd like to dedicate this book to the men and women of American Motors Corporation. In the 33 year lifespan of that outstanding company your devotion, enthusiasm, hard work and perseverance, plus your genuine belief in what you were doing were key elements that enabled AMC, against all odds, to rise to a great prominence and to set sales records which will never be broken. Be proud of what you accomplished. You made the automotive industry much more interesting—and you made history.

About the Author

Without a doubt the best-known, most prolific writer of American Motors lore is author Patrick Foster. His eight previous books are legendary: 'American Motors, The Last Independent,' 'The Metropolitan Story,' 'Mister Javelin,' 'The Nash Styling Sketchbook,' 'The Story of Jeep,' 'Super 70s - Cars of the Disco Decade,' 'Rambler 1950-1969 Photo Archive,' 'The Standard Catalog of Jeep.' Mr. Foster is considered the foremost authority on the entire family of American Motors brands—Rambler, AMC, Nash, Hudson, Jeep, etc. He also writes for the best magazines in the business—*Collectible Automobile, Forward, Special Interest Autos,* and *Automobile Quarterly* magazines. In addition, he has a regular column in *Old Cars Weekly.*

Pat Foster resides with wife Diane and daughter Caitlin in Milford, Connecticut, a lovely town on the shores of Long Island Sound, where he's often seen driving his beloved Ramblers.

Contents

This 1954 Hudson Super Wasp Hollywood hardtop has especially pleasing lines. Note the wire wheel hubcaps and Hudson's trademark roof-mounted radio antenna. The Super Wasp rode the same 119-inch wheelbase as the Wasp but came with a larger engine and was priced higher.

CHAPTER 1

In the Beginning

1954-1957

When American Motors Corporation came into being on May 1, 1954, it was an historic moment which in retrospect was one of the signal events marking the beginning of the final era for America's independent automakers.

For many years there had been two classes of automobile manufacturers. GM, Ford and Chrysler composed the predominant group known as the Big Three, while all the other companies, Auburn, Cord, Packard, Hudson, Studebaker, Crosley, Willys, Bantam, Hudson, etc., were lumped together in a group known as the independent automakers, or more simply, the Independents.

Since 1900, America had seen the rise and fall of literally hundreds of small auto companies; Knox, Kissel, Sears, Apperson, Stutz, Moon, Durant, the list went on and on. Most of the small automakers that survived the early shakeout of the industry were fairly prosperous in the mid-1920s, because America's stock market was soaring and there was plenty of money around. However, after the stock market crashed in 1929 the ensuing Great Depression killed off many of the remaining independents. The gradual economic recovery of the 1930s saw the ranks of the independents thinned to just a handful. Some of these, most notably Willys-Overland, probably would have failed too, if World War II had not brought a flood of orders for defense products.

By war's end there were just a few large independents left. Packard, Willys-Overland, Hudson, Studebaker, Nash and Crosley were joined by a new company, Kaiser-Frazer. Because no cars had been produced from early 1942 to late 1945, after the war there was an immense pent-up demand for new cars, and all the companies,

especially the independents, enjoyed easy sales and good profits. Automakers could sell virtually every car they could build. In fact, from 1945 to 1947 the only problem automakers faced was trying to boost production to meet demands.

This happy scenario began to end in mid-1948, as production finally began to catch up with the backlog of demand. By 1949 sales were harder to come by and dealers began to discount prices to spur demand. The early 1950s brought the Korean War and with it a new upsurge. In 1953 the tide turned again and demand fell sharply. When it did, the Big Three began to push harder for sales. Profit margins fell.

Over the previous seven years labor costs had gone up dramatically as a result of companies giving in to union demands in order to avoid costly strikes. But the biggest single factor that brought a disproportionate harm to the independents was the skyrocketing cost of tooling for new models. The increased expense hurt the small makers more than the Big Three because although it cost Hudson the same to tool up a new car as it cost Ford, Hudson would amortize the cost over, say, 80,000 to 100,000 cars per year, while Ford could spread the costs over perhaps a million cars, thus reducing its per-car cost. Faced with that sort of disadvantage it was easy to see that sooner or later the independents would go out of business. This problem had been of less consequence while sales were strong and margins high but now that sales were down the problems rose to the surface and they had to be dealt with.

The only option for the smaller automakers was to merge in order that they might reap the benefits of greater production and better amortization.

The merger of The Hudson Motor Car Company and Nash-Kelvinator Corporation took place on May 1, 1954, after many months of negotiation and preparations. During the year the two firms continued to manufacture competing small cars, the Nash Rambler (top) and the Hudson Jet (bottom).

The year 1954 was last year Hudson would offer a convertible in the senior line. This 1954 Hudson Hornet shows the beauty of these last full-size Hudson convertibles. Note the gorgeous lines and beautiful wire wheel covers. Beginning in 1955 the only Hudson convertible would be the tiny Metropolitan.

Willys-Overland led the way in 1953, merging with Kaiser. That same year Nash-Kelvinator president George Mason proposed a merger of his firm with Packard and Hudson, hoping to create a three-make company wherein all three brands would share a common body shell. His plan was by far the best one for all parties involved but in the end Packard management decided against making their company a part of the new combine. Mason wasn't interested in merging with Studebaker or Kaiser; so he decided to merge his firm with Hudson only.

The deal had been rumored in mid-1953, and openly discussed later in the year. In June 1953, Mason and A. E. Barit, CEO of Hudson met to discuss the possibility of a merger. Over several talks they hammered out an agreement. On January 14, 1954, the consolidation plan was approved by directors of both Hudson and Nash, and later approved by a vote of the stockholders of both companies. The merger officially went into effect May 1, 1954, and the name of the new company was American Motors Corporation. Its chief executive, George Walter Mason, was one of the smartest auto executives on the planet. With Mason at the wheel stockholders knew that AMC was in good hands. Second in command was

Mason's handpicked successor, George Wilcken Romney, the hard-working, talented and well-liked former executive vice president of Nash-Kelvinator who now took the same position in the new firm.

American Motors was, as corporations go, a rather large company. At its inception it was the fourth largest automaker in America. AMC, comprised of three main divisions, Nash, Hudson and Kelvinator, had over 40,000 employees, more than 58,000 stockholders, and over 10,000 dealers (including appliance dealers) in more than 100 countries. It operated plants in five states and 44 cities around the world. In the prior 50 years Nash and Hudson had produced over six million cars and ten million appliances.

One of the saving graces of the merger was the similarity in products; Nash and Hudson senior cars were big, comfortable machines that sold in the medium price range. Although they didn't compete directly against each other they were similar in size, so future models of each could easily be produced from a common body shell, yielding tremendous savings. There was a problem in the small car category, however. Nash had its compact Rambler model, which competed with the similar Hudson Jet. The Rambler was a sales

Big Hudsons for 1954 got revised styling up front. The hood and hood scoop were altered, and new bumper guards fitted. The grille was completely new, and looked somewhat like the intake scoop on a jet.

appreciable volume and both were virtually hand-built so whatever happened to them would have little impact on the corporation's sales figures.

Because the merger took place midyear both companies continued to sell their existing products. For Hudson this would be the final year that the cars they offered would be 'pure Hudson.'

Although they continued offering the same cars they had been selling, in 1954 Hudson dealers got an additional model–the first new Hudson to arrive as a result of the merger. These were English-built Metropolitans fitted with Hudson grille badges. Priced at $1,445 for the hardtop and $1,469 for the convertible, the Hudson Metropolitans were not big sellers but they provided dealers an additional product to sell, one which appealed to import buyers.

During 1954 Hudson dealers still offered the Jet compact. Comfortable and sturdily built, the 105-inch wheelbase Hudson Jet was a nice car that unfortunately just didn't fit into Mason's plans. Part of the problem was a matter of costs; an outside supplier produced the Jet's body shell, whereas the Rambler's was built in the company's own plants. That, plus the fact that the Rambler was better known by the public, and it sold better, sealed the Jet's fate.

Next up in price were the Hudson Wasp and Super Wasp, both on a 119-inch wheelbase. The Wasps were offered in two- and four-door sedans, a club coupe, Hollywood hardtop coupe and a very attractive convertible. These were big cars priced to compete in the lower medium price range. The pinnacle of the Hudson line was the powerful,

success; the Jet hadn't done well in the two years it had been offered. Since there wasn't enough sales volume to permit marketing two compacts under separate nameplates, Mason decided that Hudson and Nash would both sell the Rambler. The Jet was discontinued.

Both car divisions also sold sports models. The Hudson Italia was a limited production sports tourer, while the Nash-Healey was a more traditional hardtop sports car (in earlier years it had offered a convertible but for 1954 Nash-Healey was available solely as a hardtop). Neither car sold in any

The most-talked about Hudson in 1954 was the limited production Hudson Italia, so-named because the cars were assembled in Italy. Production began during the summer of 1954 and only 26 were produced.

Nash offered a special limited production car in 1954, the beautiful Nash-Healey sports car. Styling was by Pininfarina. Built on a chassis assembled in England by Donald Healey using a Nash Ambassador six-cylinder engine and manual transmission, final assembly took place in Pininfarina's shops in Italy.

race-proven Hudson Hornet series offered in club coupe, Hollywood hardtop coupe, four-door sedan, and two-door convertible styles. New this year was a Hornet Special series slotted in between the Super Wasp and Hornet models. Hudson also had its specialty Italia sports coupe this year, though only 26 of these were built.

Like Hudson, Nash's lowest priced car for 1954 was the Metropolitan. The little Met had debuted in March of that year, the first small import to be sold by an American company. George Mason of Nash felt that a significant market existed among families for a second new car, and he believed women would prefer something small, economical and inexpensive to buy. The Nash Mets were priced the same as the Hudson Mets, and were identical in every detail save the badges.

Nash's famed Rambler was the next step up on the price ladder; it wasn't a big step either. Although Rambler's 100-inch wheelbase models had traditionally been offered in premium body types—convertibles, hardtops and station wagons—for 1954 Nash brought Rambler's base price down by adding a two-door sedan priced at

Nash introduced its new Metropolitan car in mid-1954. Built on an 85-inch wheelbase and powered by an Austin A-40 four-cylinder engine, the Metropolitan was a tiny two-passenger car aimed at singles and families needing an economical second car. After AMC was formed a 1954 Hudson Metropolitan debuted. It was the first new Hudson to arrive as a result of the merger of the two companies.

The Nash Rambler convertible for 1954. This was the last time a convertible would be offered in the Nash Rambler line-up. Another Rambler convertible wouldn't be seen until 1961, four years after the Nash name was discontinued.

The big news in the Rambler line for 1954 was the addition of four-door models on a longer 108-inch wheelbase. The increased wheelbase meant that the new Ramblers were much roomier—a size that later would be considered mid-sized rather than compact. The bigger Rambler models sold surprisingly well.

only $1,550 in Deluxe trim, which was just $105 more than a Metropolitan hardtop. This made Rambler the lowest-priced six-cylinder family car on the market. Rambler this year also added a beautiful four-door Cross Country station wagon, and a four-door sedan, both on a longer 108-inch wheelbase. The new larger Ramblers sold very well, indicating a preferrence for cars with more room than the 100-inch Ramblers offered.

The senior Nash line included the Statesman, a big, roomy car on a 114-inch wheelbase powered by a 195.6 cid flathead six. It was a tad underpowered for that horsepower-crazed era but it was good on gas and as comfortable as a car could be. The Statesman line consisted of two- and four-door sedans plus a two-door hardtop. The top of the Nash sedan line was the Ambassador, a stately looking machine on a 121-inch wheelbase. Like most Nash cars the Ambassador was powered by a six-cylinder engine, in this case a 252.6 cid in-line mill that was one of the sturdiest, smoothest engines on

Nash Statesman Super for 1954. The Statesman was the middle of the Nash range, a full-size car that offered better economy than other big cars. This year a new grille and new headlamp rings offered improved styling.

the planet. The Ambassador line offered the same body styles as the Statesman.

Nash-Healey returned for its fourth year on the market, offered in a single hardtop coupe style and powered by the big Ambassador six.

In October 1954 CEO George Mason died quite unexpectedly. The board of directors quickly elevated George Romney to president and CEO. Romney was energetic and he swiftly turned to the task of shaping the direction of the new company.

In the midst of trying to combine two industrial firms while struggling to compete with both Chevrolet and Ford, who were locked in a brutal

Big Nash Ambassador for 1954. Although this was the third year this body was in production it still looked remarkably good. Improvements this year included a new grille and headlamp rings. The continental spare tire mount was standard on all Ambassador and Statesman Custom models that year.

40 Million Miles of Raves!
The Amazing Success Story
of America's Entirely
New Kind of Car

1955 *Metropolitan*

For 1955 the Nash Metropolitan looked the same as the previous year. Hudson dealers again offered a Hudson Metropolitan, which was identical to the Nash with the exception of the grille badge.

shell. Unlike the Nashes the Hudsons had open wheel wells, and only a few exterior sheet metal pieces were shared. To help maintain Hudson's uniqueness Hudson engines were used in the new cars rather than Nash engines. The former 'Step-down' Hudsons, which had been sold since 1948 with only minor styling updates, were dropped.

Nash, meanwhile, got a complete restyling with new exterior sheet metal and front-end styling that featured headlamps mounted in the grille—a very unusual look indeed. The two-door sedans were dropped from the senior line and horsepower was upped a bit. Like Hudson's Italia, the Nash-Healey was dropped, though apparently some leftover 1954s were re-titled as 1955s.

The big Hudsons and the big Nashes both got a new engine choice this year, a potent 208 hp, 320 cid V8 built by Packard, offered only in conjunction with a Packard Twin Ultramatic transmission. The market was shunning six-cylinder medium priced cars, so it was hoped the new V8 would spark a sales increase.

For 1955 both car divisions sold Rambler, the only difference being the nameplates. Ramblers had new styling in the form of a new egg crate grille and new front fenders with the wheels opened up. Sales increased dramatically so although the company posted another loss of almost $7 million

sales war, American Motors' sales tumbled and the company declared a loss of just over $11 million for its first year of business. A loss had been expected, so no one was overly concerned about it.

For 1955 AMC was able to introduce all-new Hudson models. They were big, good-looking cars based on the existing Nash senior line body

The Hudson Jet wasn't offered in 1955. Instead, Hudson dealers offered a complete line of Ramblers, identical to the Nash products with the exception of nameplates and grille badges. In this press photo the car has generic 'R' hubcaps and its grille badge is almost unnoticeable so that both Hudson and Nash dealers could use it in advertisements.

it didn't raise many red flags. That loss was much less than the prior year and things seemed to be moving in the right direction.

But one problem was apparent—AMC's big cars weren't selling as well as they should have. The only bright spot on the sales charts was the Rambler—it was hot! Faced with dwindling cash reserves, George Romney decided to spend his product dollars on an all-new Rambler. Originally planned as a 1957 model, he ordered that it be ready for a 1956 introduction.

The 1956 Rambler was a sensation! Clean-lined and modern, it looked like no other car ever had. AMC's styling director Edmund Anderson gave it large window areas for a light airy feel, big wheel openings, slab sides that made it look larger and more important, all on the longer 108-inch wheelbase that buyers preferred. Response was terrific, though sales were held down by various problems related to the year-early introduction.

Meanwhile sales of the senior Hudson and Nash cars continued to fall. Nash Ambassador and Statesman models this year got reshaped rear fenders, new 'lollypop' tail lamps and, midyear, bold front fender moldings. Hudsons got a complete facelift highlighted by a dramatic new grille. The Packard-built V8 was larger this year, 352 cid and 220 hp. Midyear brought new Hornet Specials and Ambassador Specials, which used the shorter 114-inch body and a new 250 cid V8, designed and built by AMC. The Specials

Here's the Rambler Country Club hardtop coupe for 1955. It wears Rambler hubcaps and no grille badge. Often even the press releases were generic in nature, referring to the car only as a Rambler without identifying it as a Nash or Hudson product.

were very attractively priced and would have sold well if the market hadn't turned its back on the independent makers. But it had. The only thing selling with any appreciable success at either division was the Rambler. With sales down yet again the company ended 1956 with a horrific loss of nearly $20 million, an incredible figure for that decade. George Romney was worried but, in typical fashion, believed he could rally the troops for one final, all-out effort to alter the downward course AMC was on.

At the introduction of the 1957 models Romney exhorted his dealers to spare no effort.

This is the Nash Rambler four-door Custom sedan for 1955, identifiable by the grille badge. This year all Ramblers got new grilles and revised front fenders with big wheel openings.

The handsome Rambler four-door Cross Country station wagon for 1955. With the addition of the new four-door models (in 1954) and added sales efforts of the Hudson dealer group, Rambler sales began to accelerate in 1955.

Nash senior cars were face-lifted for 1955, gaining new front fenders with a raised wheel opening; a racy one-piece grille with inset headlamps inspired by the Nash-Healey. To ensure oncoming drivers could gauge the Nash's width even in darkness, delicate guide lamps were placed in the leading edge of front fenders.

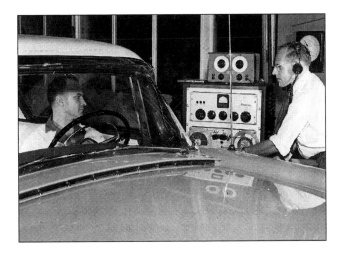

Nash engineer Richard Kishline (right) runs some sound tests on a 1955 model senior Nash. The man at the wheel is unidentified.

Amazingly, even though the merger of Nash and Hudson didn't take place until May of 1954 the newly formed American Motors Corporation unveiled completely new Hudson senior cars later that same year!

Here's the very attractive Hudson Wasp for 1955. Although the big Hudsons were based on the Nash body shell the Hudson senior cars retained the Wasp and Hornet names and continued to offer the famed Hudson six-cylinder engines. A new Packard-built V8 debuted in the Hornet series.

During 1956 Metropolitans continued to wear Nash or Hudson grille badges, though this was the final year they would do so. AMC asked journalists to stop referring to the car by brand, suggesting they refer to it as the "Metropolitan - from American Motors."

Every sale, he declared, was vital. He urged each dealer to pledge to sell just one more car each month than they had in the prior year—that, he insisted, would bring AMC to profitability. Next, he gathered his factory workers together and implored them to work harder than ever to produce cars of the highest quality. To all these people whose livelihoods depended on American Motors, he stated, "I firmly believe that our tide has turned. We are in league with the future, and 1957 should be the bright beginning of that more prosperous future."

Sales of AMC's big cars collapsed. Evidently the public was no longer interested in medium priced cars from non-Big Three companies. The only thing they would buy from an independent dealer was something they couldn't get elsewhere—and that was the Rambler. Its sales rose slowly, but towards the end of the model year it became apparent that Rambler had taken hold. Dealers were running out of cars and the factory couldn't keep up with the sudden increase in demand. Although the company reported a loss of $11.8 million for the year, 1958 was bound to be the comeback year.

Ramblers were all new for 1956. The slower selling two-door 100-inch wheelbase models were dropped. All Ramblers now were four-door models on a 108-inch wheelbase. The Rambler hardtop four-door Custom was particularly attractive.

AMC debuted another industry first this year—the hardtop station wagon, the most expensive model in the Rambler line-up. Ramblers continued to be sold under both Nash and Hudson nameplates, though this was the final year they would be marketed that way.

There were some minor styling refinements to the senior Nash line for 1956. New rear fenders with big 'lollipop' tail lamps raised the rear fender line, while larger running lights adorned the front fenders. This is the Statesman for 1956, which was available this year in a single four-door model in Super trim.

Here the new front running lamps can be more easily seen. Nash Ambassadors got revised trim this year, with several running changes made during the model year. The young boy standing in the driveway looks very proud of his parent's neat Ambassador Country Club hardtop.

One big change occurred midway through the 1956 model year when Nash introduced a new Ambassador Special series. These used the Statesman body with the new American Motors 250 cid V8 engine under the hood. Pricing started as low as $2,355 for a four-door Super sedan, while this Country Club hardtop was priced at $2,462.

Like Hudson, Nash offered a Packard-built V8 on its big Ambassadors. But because of the high cost of these engines the V8 senior Nashes were priced rather high and sales were slow.

Big Hudsons had a new appearance this year. Called V-line styling, it consisted of a new grille, revised side trim and lots of added chrome. This Hudson Hornet Custom for 1956 wears a three-tone paint job.

Here's the Hudson Hornet Hollywood hardtop for 1956. Small fins were attached to the top of both the front and rear fenders to make them look a bit different from the prior year's models.

Here are four models offered by American Motors in 1956, seen at that year's Mobilgas Economy run. The Rambler was placed in a separate 'limited displacement' class so that its superior fuel economy wouldn't embarrass the Big Three family cars. Rambler that year placed first in overall gas mileage during the run.

American Motors' future was up in the air at the beginning of 1957. Company president George Romney exhorted dealers to bend every effort to sell cars, declaring, "We cannot have another year like 1956 in 1957 and survive—we cannot." Here, a 1957 Rambler Super is seen undergoing testing.

The fastest American sedan in 1957 was the Rambler Rebel. Powered by a new AMC-built 327 cid V8, only about 1,500 of these limited production Rambler muscle cars were built. Rambler became a separate make this year and was no longer badged as a Hudson or a Nash.

A tremendously popular model for 1957 was this Rambler Super four-door station wagon, bought by thousands of American families. Optional two-tone paint and full wheel covers give a very luxurious look.

The price leader of the Rambler line for 1957 was this Deluxe four-door sedan. Priced at just $1,961, it was marketed as the perfect business car. The white wall tires, full wheel discs and two-tone paint were optional at extra cost.

For 1957 the Nash line consisted of only the Ambassador on a 121-inch wheelbase. Four models were offered, a two-door hardtop and a four-door sedan in either Super or Custom trim. This is the Super hartop.

All Ambassadors this year had eight-cylinder engines, using the new AMC-built 327 cid, 255 horsepower V8. Shown is the handsome Ambassador Custom hardtop.

For its final year on the market the big Nash got revised styling including a lower roof, new front fenders with full wheel cutouts, and quad headlamps. Nash was the first car with four headlamps on all models.

Hudson Hornet made its final appearance in 1957. Styling changes this year were minimal. Hudsons carried AMC's new 327 V8 on all models sold in the U.S., though a small number of six-cylinder senior Hudsons were produced for overseas markets.

The powerful and pretty 1957 Hudson Hornet marked the end of a long-running and well-regarded brand.

The Rambler American two-door sedan offered a very low price—$1,789 for a Deluxe model and $1,874 in Super trim. Only two-door sedans were offered in the American series during 1958.

CHAPTER 2

Rambler to the Forefront

1958-1965

When American Motors announced its 1958 cars George Romney felt pleased and confident. He was certain that AMC had turned the corner and that this year would see the company report its first-ever annual profit. Rambler sales began to climb during the spring of 1957, set new monthly sales records for May and June, and sales continued to grow.

The exhilarating sales momentum would be helped in 1958 by a number of factors. The Rambler Six and V8 models were given new front and rear styling for a more modern look, and were joined by a new 100-inch wheelbase Rambler American priced at a bargain $1,789. This newest Rambler was in fact a reintroduction of the 1955 Rambler two-door sedan, a bold move decided on by Romney. With this new small Rambler dealers could boast offering the lowest-priced car made in America, and it was certain to add incremental sales.

The high performance, limited-production Rebel wasn't offered this year but the Rambler V8 models were renamed Rambler Rebels, although they carried the smaller 250 cid V8 rather than the fire-breathing 327 cid V8.

AMC, which just one year earlier had offered four automotive brands, was down to just two this year: Rambler and Metropolitan. The Nash and Hudson names were dropped, and AMC's big car now was built on a Rambler chassis stretched to a 117-inch wheelbase. Dubbed the 'Ambassador by Rambler,' rather than the Rambler Ambassador, it was equipped with the big AMC 327 cid V8 and was a plush, comfortable 'compact' big car. Sales of all AMC cars climbed this year, a sign that the public was being won over to the AMC standard.

Romney continued on the same course for 1959, with even greater results. Not much was really new. The big Ramblers received refinements plus some minor restyling of the rear doors and trim. A two-door station wagon was added to the Rambler American line-up. The Metropolitan series got a host of improvements this year, including a long overdue opening trunk lid, side vent windows and larger tires. A one-piece rear window had debuted in mid-1958. Like its Rambler stable mate, Met sales reached a new height this year. Although the sum total of American Motors' new product changes was small, the public flocked to AMC dealers and sales skyrocketed. The company reported production of 374,240 cars in the 1959 model year.

For 1960 AMC added a 100-inch wheelbase four-door sedan to the Rambler American line, greatly expanding the small Rambler's appeal. Midyear brought new Custom models that offered the more-powerful AMC overhead valve six-cylinder engine in place of the standard flathead six, plus twin horns, oil bath air cleaner, Custom upholstery, Custom steering wheel and full wheel discs.

The Metropolitan series, oddly enough, got almost nothing new. The Met's enclosed wheels, continental spare tire carrier and 1950s style two-tone paint treatment were beginning to look out of date by 1960 and it's surprising that AMC didn't at least offer Mets in solid colors, or with updated styling. The company was neglecting its little import car.

The big Ramblers had trimmer rooflines, slim 'C' pillars, plus cleaner styling up front. Rear fenders were reshaped to reduce the size of the fins, which were now canted to the side. Body

Metropolitan sales were up strongly for 1958 as Americans began to embrace the idea of smaller cars. Like Rambler, Metropolitan became a separate make in 1957. AMC reported a profit of $26 million for 1958.

side moldings were new. All these minor touches kept the senior Ramblers looking up to date. A new three-seat version of the station wagon was introduced. It was considered a five-door, because instead of a conventional dropdown tailgate, it featured a side-opening rear door.

American Motors continued to find success with its Rambler line-up in 1960. Net sales surpassed the $1 billion mark for the first time,

an incredible accomplishment for a company that was nearly bankrupt just three years earlier. Profits for the year were $48 million. AMC reported production of 458,841 cars for the model year, of which a bit more than 120,000 were in the smaller American series. Rambler by this time was ranked fourth among U.S. car makes.

The company had a lot of news for 1961. First, the big Rambler Six and Rebel V8 models were

Midway through the 1958 model year Metropolitan hardtops got a new one-piece rear window, replacing the former three-pane window seen here. Imported cars were selling in increasing numbers so this was a good year for Metropolitan dealers.

AMC reintroduced the former 100-inch wheelbase Ramblers at the beginning of the 1958 model year. Now dubbed the Rambler American, these two-door sedans were very popular. This is the first Rambler American coming off the assembly line.

consolidated into one series called the Rambler Classic. Although these cars continued to use the same body shell introduced in 1956, a restyling of the front end went a long way in keeping it looking fresh and new. Headlamps were now lower, flanking an expensive-looking new grille. New front fenders and a new hood created a new 'eyebrow' styling theme for the front end, and side moldings were new.

The big Ambassador series didn't share the Classics' new styling, instead getting all-new front-end styling that was very European looking. Although the eyebrow theme was evident, Ambassador had a completely different, more luxurious style.

There was even bigger news in the small Rambler line. Gone was the rounded '1950s' styling which the Rambler American had featured since its resurrection in 1958. However, the American's new look for 1961 wasn't a complete redesign, only an extensive restyling of the existing car. American Motors stylists under styling director Ed Anderson designed all-new sheet metal to hide the old Nash Rambler underbody. It was a relatively inexpensive re-skinning of an old shell, and as

The senior Rambler models for 1958 had restyled front and rear fenders, new grilles, and quad headlamps.

such it was surprisingly effective. It appeared to be an all-new car. The tightly drawn lines and reduced overhangs made the Rambler American even more compact than before, although of course it retained the same interior room and identical 100-inch wheelbase as before. Along with the new styling AMC added some new models. Best-looking was a sharp two-door convertible, a really

Ramblers on the 108-inch wheelbase came in two series for 1958—Rambler Six and Rambler Rebel V8. Beginning in 1958 Rebels used the smaller 250 cid V8 rather than the 327 V8 seen in the 1957 models. This Rebel V8 station wagon even has air conditioning, as indicated by the small emblem on the front door.

The former Nash and Hudson big cars were not offered for 1958, but in their place was a new "Ambassador by Rambler," which used the basic Rambler body shell on a longer 117-inch wheelbase. All Ambassadors included as standard equipment the AMC 327 cid V8.

attractive, youthful-looking machine that was the lowest-priced ragtop from a U.S. producer that year. More practical, perhaps, was the new American four-door station wagon, which with its squared-off roof offered more useful space than before. The American line continued to offer the 90 hp flathead six as standard equipment on Deluxe and Super models. The 125 hp overhead valve six-cylinder engine was standard on Custom Americans and, new this year, optional on the Deluxe and Super series.

Once again the imported Metropolitans saw no real changes or improvements. It was affecting their sales, which had peaked in 1959, with 14,959 retailed that year. Sales had fallen to 11,689 for 1960, disappointing but still acceptable. However, for 1961 only 8,881 Mets were retailed, and it was becoming plain that the company was losing interest in its littlest product.

Here's something you don't see very often—the optional air coil suspension offered on senior Rambler models. It certainly caught the interest of these men.

Because right-hand steering Metropolitans were already being produced for the British market it was simple to send some over to the U.S. where they could be used by police departments for parking patrol. The Fairlawn, New Jersey police department purchased this 1959 model.

AMC's sales fell in 1961 due to overall softness in the market. Net earnings dropped drastically to $23 million as the company was forced to spend more money marketing its cars in a tough sales environment.

Model year 1962 saw a consolidation of the AMC line. The old 'Ambassador by Rambler' nomenclature was abandoned as the senior AMC car was now referred to as the Rambler Ambassador. This year the Ambassador also abandoned its longer wheelbase, and was built on the same 108-inch wheelbase as the Rambler Classic. In a reversal of 1961's strategy, styling differences between the two cars were minimal.

Metropolitans got several needed improvements midway through the 1959 model year. A trunk lid was introduced, along with vent windows. Met's popularity continued to grow this year.

Metropolitans continued to be offered in just two models for 1959, the two-door hardtop and this two-door convertible. The Met ragtop was the only convertible offered by American Motors from 1955 to 1960.

The popular Rambler American two-door sedan returned for 1959 with minimal appearance changes. American Motors was enjoying tremendous sales growth this year as buyers flocked to showrooms.

However, Classics for 1962 were offered only as six-cylinder models. Ambassador prices were reduced and production almost doubled, as Ambassador now served as AMC's sole V8 line.

All Ramblers benefited from a new twin circuit brake system, a safety improvement so important that by 1967 the federal government made it mandatory equipment on all cars. Aside from Rambler only a handful of the most expensive cars in the world—among them Rolls-Royce and some top-line Cadillac models—had these brakes in 1962. Required engine oil change intervals were increased to 4,000 miles on all Ramblers this year, and AMC's new 'Power-Guard 24' battery came with a two-year warranty. The ceramic armored muffler and tailpipe were guaranteed for life.

All senior Ramblers got a new front suspension with a wider track, restyled rear fenders (without

A second model was added to the Rambler American line for 1959; this popular two-door station wagon priced at $2,060 in Deluxe trim and $2,145 in Super trim. AMC reported a $60 million profit for 1959.

For 1959 Rambler senior models got only mildly revised styling. A new grille was evident, along with reshaped rear doors and modified trim. This Rebel V8 four-door hardtop combined Rambler quality and economy in an especially attractive package.

fins), and a slimmer, concealed 'B' pillar. Rambler Classic added a new model—a two-door sedan offered in Deluxe, Custom and '400' trim. Although a two-door Ambassador wasn't catalogued, a small number were built.

Rambler American models got a new, more expensive-looking grille and revised trim. A new semi-automatic transmission called E-stick debuted. With it, a driver still had to shift through the gears but the clutch pedal was eliminated by a servo that operated the clutch automatically. E-stick offered drivers the gas mileage of a manual transmission combined with some of the convenience of an automatic.

Early in the year the company announced that it would cease importing Metropolitans. Although

More commonly purchased were the Rambler Rebel four-door sedans like this. American Motors set a new record in 1959 with production of 374,240 cars.

The 1959 Rebel V8 station wagon was an ideal family car, providing lots of room, power and economy. Interestingly, this press photo was taken at the home of AMC's styling director Ed Anderson. At the time Anderson owned a fairly large property in Romeo, Michigan.

The Ambassador for 1959. As in 1958, factory advertisements referred to this car as the 'Ambassador by Rambler' rather than as a Rambler Ambassador, a subtle effort to keep the Ambassador line separate from the mainstream Ramblers.

The lovely Ambassador four-door hardtop station wagon was the very summit of the American Motors product line. Only 578 of these Custom hardtop station wagons were produced for 1959, making this a rare and very desirable collector car.

Metropolitan sales fell sharply in 1960 as the public turned increasingly to the other imported cars and the Rambler American.

it had earned a decent share of the import car market in the early days, actual unit sales of Metropolitans had never amounted to a significant number. AMC wanted to focus its attention on the higher volume Ramblers, which had the advantage of being produced in the company's own plants, providing a greater profit margin. Metropolitans, once badged as Hudsons or Nashes, had been sold since 1957 as a separate make, never as a Rambler model, so for the first time since its formation AMC would be offering only one brand of cars.

CEO George Romney left AMC in 1962 after successfully running for governor of Michigan. Romney had held the company together during its darkest period, sometimes by sheer force of personality, and brought it to its greatest success, so it was very sad to see him go. To replace him the board of directors named Richard Cross as

chairman and Roy Abernethy as president.

American Motors got back on track for 1962, reporting sales of over $1 billion for the year, profits of $34 million (up 45 percent from the prior year), and a new record for unit sales. Worldwide wholesale sales of Ramblers—that is, sales to its dealers—totaled 478,132, of which 43,646 were sold outside the United States. Rambler's percentage of U.S. industry registrations was an incredible 6.7 percent.

American Motors was on a roll, and for 1963 the company had a line of completely redesigned big Ramblers to offer. The new Classic and Ambassador models rode a longer 112-inch wheelbase. Bodylines were lower, vastly more modern, and very handsome. Ed Anderson's styling team endowed the new Ramblers with large window areas to give interiors a light, airy feel,

In 1960 AMC added this attractive four-door sedan to the low-priced American series. Unlike the similar looking four-door Rambler of 1955, which was built on a 108-inch wheelbase, this car rode a 100-inch wheelbase.

The Rambler American two-door station wagon for 1960 was the lowest priced wagon on the market with a starting price of just $2,185 for a Super model, and $2,235 for a Custom model.

American Motors introduced a new aluminum block six-cylinder engine in 1960 in the senior Rambler line. Before it was offered it underwent rigorous high-speed testing on the test track. This photo shows a fleet of Ramblers equipped with the new engine undergoing durability testing.

and large wheel openings for a sporty, aggressive stance. Although compact on the outside, the new Ramblers had full-size room on the inside.

As before, Ambassador and Classic shared the same wheelbase and body with only minor differences in appearance. Both series were offered in a range of body styles including two- and four-door sedans and four-door station wagons. Ambassador now included a two-door sedan as

a regular model, but as before, neither Classic nor Ambassador offered a two-door hardtop or convertible. At introduction time Classics were available only in six-cylinder versions while Ambassadors equipped with the 327 cid engine continued to be the sole V8 models. However, midyear saw the introduction of Classic V8 models, using a new 287 cid V8 that produced 198 hp.

Rambler Americans got an expensive-looking new grille; the third new grille in as many years. The American line added a pert two-door hardtop to the range, the first hardtop American ever. Not since 1955 had AMC offered a two-door hardtop on its 100-inch wheelbase models. Because of their discontinuation in mid-1962 there wasn't a 1963 Metropolitan.

Motor Trend magazine bestowed its coveted 1963 'Car of the Year' award on the entire Rambler

One great new feature offered in the 1960 senior Rambler wagon was a side opening rear door, allowing easier entry for third seat passengers. The three-seat five-door wagon was available in Rambler Six, Rebel V8 and Ambassador models.

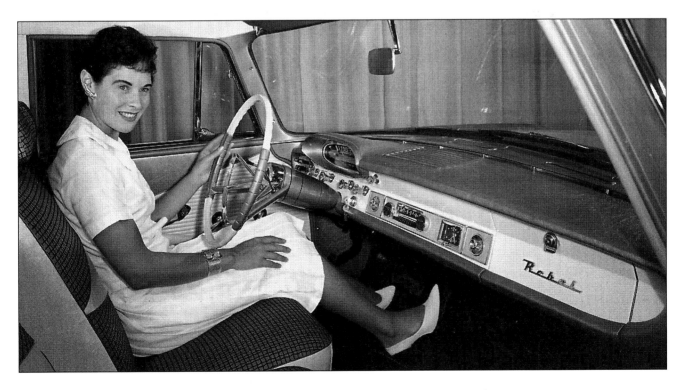

Modern Rambler features for 1960 included the individual reclining front seats, as well as head restraints, as seen in this 1960 Rambler Rebel V8. In 1960 American Motors sales exceeded $1 billion for the first time in its history.

An exceptionally popular family car for 1960 was the Rambler Six four-door sedan. The big Rambler sedans this year featured new rear fender styling and revised trim.

The Rambler Rebel V8 station wagon for 1960. Rambler's trademark 'dip' in the station wagon's rear roofline, a design feature that debuted on the 1956 models, is very noticeable in this photo.

line. Public response to the new Ramblers was literally overwhelming and the factory simply couldn't keep up with demand. For the fiscal year ending September 30, 1963, AMC reported wholesale sales (sales to dealers) of an incredible 511,038 Ramblers worldwide—the first time an independent American automaker had ever sold a half million cars in one year. Net earnings were $37 million on record sales of $1.13 billion, the third time the corporation had topped a billion in annual sales. By that point there were over 2.7 million Rambler owners in the country.

That fall the company unveiled all-new Rambler Americans for 1964. The range included two-door sedans, four-door sedans and wagons, a two-door hardtop and a convertible. Using a number of inner stampings shared with the Classic/

One of the more unusual design features of the 1960 Ambassador is the compound wraparound windshield seen here. The greatly enlarged windshield glass curved both on the sides and at the top, providing exceptional visibility.

Wouldn't you love to have one of these cars today? This is a very rare 1960 Ambassador hardtop station wagon, featuring beautiful lines and a powerful 327 cid V8.

Ambassador series, the new Americans were completely redesigned. Wheelbase was increased to 106 inches, but overall length increased just four inches. Interior room was much larger, rear seat width was increased by one foot, and rooflines were lower. Overall it was a very modern look, able to challenge the offerings of its principal competition by Ford and Chevrolet.

For 1964 Rambler Classic got a new grille and hood, plus a new two-door hardtop body style. Tilt wheel was a new option. Midyear brought an all-new 232 cid six-cylinder engine, available at first only on top line models. It was a completely new design, a lighter, more efficient engine with a sturdy seven main bearing crankshaft that would eventually replace the old 195.6 cid six. The new engine debuted in a special Classic model dubbed the Rambler Typhoon, of which just 2,520 were built. All Typhoons were two-door hardtops, painted Solar Yellow with a black roof.

Ambassador also got the new two-door hardtop body and it was a beauty. Like Classic, Ambassador received a new hood and grille, which gave it a more luxurious look for 1964. The three millionth Rambler was built during the year.

New competition from Chevrolet appeared with the Chevelle and Malibu mid-size cars. They were about the same size and price as the Rambler

The man in the center of this photo is American Motors' legendary engineer Carl Chakmakian, shown here during testing of the new AMC aluminum block six-cylinder engine. Some of the tests were run with NASCAR observers who would certify the results.

The clean, uncluttered engine compartment of this 1960 Rambler holds the new aluminum block 195.6 cid six-cylinder engine. The durability of some of these engines has been surprisingly good.

By 1961 the Metropolitan was past its prime and beginning to look out of date. Bright two-tone paint schemes and continental spare tires, so popular in the 1950s, were out of style now. Metropolitan sales fell again this year.

For 1961 American Motors stylists under the direction of Ed Anderson completely restyled the Rambler American. To reduce costs they were instructed to retain the inner body stampings of the 1950-1960 Rambler 100-inch car. However, although only the exterior body panels were retooled, the car appeared to be all new.

Classic, and were backed by Chevy's huge and very aggressive sales organization, and it hurt Rambler Classic sales badly. On the other hand, the new American sold amazingly well, which offset much of the Classic's sales drop.

Still, when the fiscal year ended and the numbers were toted up, the effects were easy to see. Dollar sales were down a bit over 10 percent, though still over the $1 billion mark. Profits fell to $26 million, still a significant piece of change but about 30 percent lower than in 1963. Total wholesale Rambler sales worldwide fell to 455,073 units.

Despite all the money that had been spent in 1963 and 1964 to bring out the all-new Ramblers, Roy Abernethy decided to overhaul his product line for 1965 to make it more competitive with the Big Three offerings. Although the basic body shell was retained, the Rambler Classic and

AMC added this very pretty convertible model to the Rambler American line for 1961. Unlike previous Rambler convertibles this one did not have fixed window frames. With a price tag of only $2,369, nearly 13,000 of these cars were sold.

Side view of the 1961 Rambler American four-door sedan shows the all-new exterior design. The thin roof panel and squared off window areas give this car a light, airy feel. It is surprisingly modern looking considering the inner body dated back to 1950.

This photo, taken during cherry blossom time in Washington, DC, shows the good looks and trim lines of the smart new American soft-top. The convertible was offered only in a single Custom model and included an overhead valve 195.6 cid six-cylinder engine in its base price.

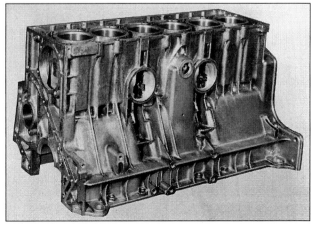

Detail photo of the six-cylinder Rambler die-cast aluminum engine block.

Rambler also introduced a new acoustical headliner for 1961 that reduced noise significantly. The new car market was down in 1961 and Rambler sales slowed with it. Profits for the year fell to $23 million.

Ambassador received completely new exterior styling for 1965.

Rambler Classic looked much bigger this year. Styling VP Dick Teague, who replaced Ed Anderson in 1962, gave the Classic a wider, more prominent grille, longer rear fenders, and more slab-sided bodylines. The effect was amazing—the Rambler Classic looked all new. A sharp convertible joined the line-up, and a 199 cid version of new six-cylinder became the standard engine in the Classic 550 series. All other Classics got the 232 cid six as standard.

Rambler Ambassador likewise had new styling, and it was markedly different from the Classics. The body sides were similar to its less expensive brethren, but Ambassador's front fenders were unique, with a pointed front edge and quad headlamps. Rear fenders were similar to Classics but unique taillights were fitted. The Ambassador convertible was especially attractive.

Rambler American, all new in 1964, received only a modified grille for 1965. The 232 cid six became available as an option, though the 195.5 cid six, offered in flathead and OHV versions, remained standard equipment.

In February the company announced the new Rambler Marlin, a sporty two-door fastback intermediate-sized car. Marlin had originally been conceived as a pony car on the smaller Rambler American shell, and actually appeared

For 1961 an effort was made to further separate the Ambassador line from the Ramblers. Ambassadors this year received completely new front-end styling with a vaguely European look. Sales, however, didn't increase and, in fact, dropped slightly.

All Ambassadors this year were of the post-sedan type, meaning that no hardtop models were produced. In all, less than 20,000 Ambassadors were produced for 1961.

as a concept car at auto shows months before the Ford Mustang debuted. The show car, known as the Tarpon, dazzled the crowds and likely would have sold well had it gone into production as an inexpensive sport coupe. Plymouth's Barracuda, which arrived later, was similar to the Tarpon and it enjoyed good sales. However, Roy Abernethy would only okay it if it could offer V8 power, which was not available on the Rambler American at that time. Abernethy ordered the Tarpon redesigned on the Classic chassis, and introduced it as the Marlin. Among the many regrettable actions he made during his tenure as president, this was one of Abernethy's more unfortunate.

The public wasn't looking for a mid-sized sporty car back then. Something like Ford's Mustang was what the market wanted—a small, sporty, compact car that could be optioned into a fire-breathing sports car, a low-buck commuter, a secretary's sports car—precisely the markets where Rambler could have made real inroads. As it

AMC continued to win accolades for outstanding fuel economy. The company competed in several different fuel economy runs with all of its models, including this 1961 Ambassador sedan.

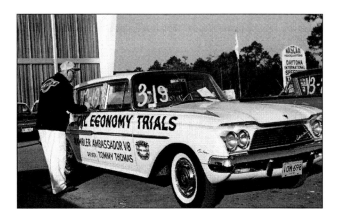

A 1961 Ambassador Custom sedan. Many of the fuel economy runs, such as this Pure Oil Economy Trial, were sanctioned by NASCAR, whose observers certified the mileage and carried out inspections to make sure rules were followed to the letter.

was, the Marlin was a flop, selling only 10,327 cars that year. Ford, by way of comparison, produced over half a million 1965 Mustangs.

For the year sales fell again, to $990 million; and profits dropped to just $5.2 million. Worldwide unit sales of Ramblers fell to just 412,736. In a move that signaled the beginning of the end for the Rambler nameplate, Roy Abernethy revealed that beginning in 1966 Ambassador and Marlin models would no longer be branded as Ramblers. In the 15 years since the modern Rambler had debuted it had built up a solid reputation and excellent name awareness, and had very loyal customers as well. With this announcement Roy Abernethy was walking away from all that brand equity, hoping to establish a new image for the company's products. The result would be disastrous for American Motors.

The lowest priced family model in the Rambler American series for 1962 was this two-door sedan in basic Deluxe trim, which sold for $1,846. American Motors also offered a two-door business sedan at slightly less cost but these were considered commercial cars and not shown in the regular sales catalog.

The Rambler American four-door station wagon was a popular model with young families. Rambler's compact size, excellent fuel economy and low price—just $2,190 for a Custom wagon—were an unbeatable combination.

Unlike the senior Rambler wagon the Rambler American continued to use an old style drop-down tailgate with transom-type lift-up rear window. The round tail lamps were a popular styling touch in the 1960s.

Although the continental spare tire mount was going out of style some aftermarket accessory companies continued to offer it. Here we see a very rare photo of a 1962 Rambler American four-door sedan with an aftermarket spare tire mount and extended rear bumper.

The author once owned a 1962 Rambler American such as this and remembers it as smooth riding, easy handling, and a great joy to drive.

The 1962 Rambler American line included three four-door sedans; a basic Deluxe priced at $1,895, a Custom at $1,958 and a top-line 400 series at $2,089. Note the restyled grille for 1962.

Part of the American Motors exhibit at the Paris Auto Show was this good-looking 1962 Rambler Classic Cross Country station wagon in Custom trim. Rambler's compact size and outstanding fuel economy made it a popular car in overseas markets.

Another 1962 Rambler Classic Custom, this one a four-door sedan. All Classics this year were six-cylinder models, as Ambassadors became the sole V8 offerings. All Rambler models this year got a new twin circuit brake system that was vastly superior to other family cars. Only Rolls-Royce and some top-line Cadillac models offered similar brake systems.

A truckload of finished Rambler bodies. Rambler bodies were manufactured at an AMC plant in Milwaukee and then trucked down to Kenosha for final assembly.

The 1962 Rambler Classic four-door sedan and station wagon. Senior Ramblers got a new front suspension, a wider front track, restyled rear fenders without fins, and a slim, concealed 'B' pillar.

For 1962 the 'Ambassador by Rambler' nomenclature was abandoned and AMC's most expensive car was now called the Rambler Ambassador. This year the Ambassador also abandoned its longer wheelbase, and was built on the same 108-inch wheelbase as the Rambler Classic.

A typical Rambler dealer's parts department. Note the 'Rambler Parts-Accessories' signs. Reproductions of these signs are still available today and popular with Rambler enthusiasts.

The clean lines of this 1963 Rambler American two-door sedan are still appealing even 40-plus years later. Since AMC ceased importing Metropolitans after 1962, the American was now the lowest priced AMC car.

For 1963 the American got a very elegant new grille. The two-door American station wagon was priced at just $2,081 in 220 trim, or $2,141 in 330 trim.

For 1963 a sporty two-door hardtop model was added to the Rambler American line. It would be the only year this body style was offered in the 100-inch American. The hardtop was available in 440 and 440H trim.

In 1963 the only convertible offered in the Rambler line was the American, and as before it was offered in a single top-line 440 model, priced at $2,344. Worldwide wholesale sales of Ramblers—that's sales to its dealers—totaled 478,132, of which 43,646 were sold outside the United States. Rambler's percentage of U.S. industry registrations was an incredible 6.7 percent.

The big Ramblers were completely restyled for 1963 under the supervision of styling director Ed Anderson. The new Classic (above; shown front and rear) and Ambassador models rode a longer 112-inch wheelbase. Bodylines were lower and vastly more modern.

At introduction time Classics were available only in six-cylinder versions while Ambassadors equipped with the 327 cid engine continued to be the sole V8 models. However, midyear saw the introduction of Classic V8 models, using a new 287 cid V8 that produced 198 horsepower.

Ed Anderson's styling team endowed the new Ramblers with large window areas to give interiors a light, airy feel, and large wheel openings for a sporty, aggressive stance. Although compact on the outside, the new Ramblers had full-size room on the inside.

Twin stick transmission was an interesting option. One stick controlled the overdrive, the other the conventional three-speed transmission. Motor Trend magazine bestowed its coveted 1963 'Car of the Year' award on the entire Rambler line.

In 1963 the new senior Ramblers introduced curved side glass to popular priced cars, a feature still used today on virtually all cars. Public response to the new Ramblers was overwhelming—AMC couldn't keep up with demand.

Three views of the handsome 1963 Rambler Ambassador Cross Country station wagon in 880 series trim. The V-grille is similar to that seen on the Classics.

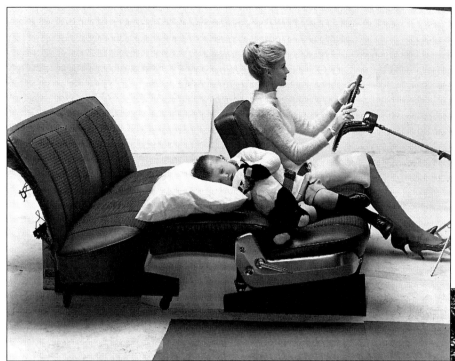

The Rambler feature that probably most people remember is the reclining seats that could be turned into a bed. They're additional proof of AMC's tremendous innovation and pioneering of new ideas. After all, virtually every car built today has reclining seats. Note the young boy is wearing a seat belt—a feature Nash introduced in 1951!

Following up the all-new 1963 big Ramblers was an all-new Rambler American for 1964. Many of the underbody stampings were shared between the two lines. Top of the American line was this very pretty convertible.

The new Rambler American series included a sharp hardtop model. As before, the hardtop was limited to the 440 and 440H top-line trim series. Wheelbase of the new American was increased to 106 inches, but overall length increased just four inches.

The new American station wagon got a roll-down rear window like larger Ramblers. For 1964 AMC's dollar sales were down a bit over 10 percent, though still passing the $1 billion mark. Profits fell to $26 million, about 30 percent lower than in 1963. Total wholesale Rambler sales worldwide fell to 455,073 units.

Interior room on the new Americans for 1964 was greatly increased. Rear seat width was increased by a foot, and rooflines were lower. The overall design was much more modern than the previous series. The three millionth Rambler was built during the year.

AMC introduced its all-new 232 cid six-cylinder engine for 1964, debuting it in the limited production Rambler Typhoon two-door hardtop. All 2,520 Typhoons built that year were painted Solar Yellow with a black roof.

Rambler Ambassador for 1964 received a new grille, a new hood and other styling updates. A very attractive two-door hardtop joined the Ambassador line-up.

Like its more expensive brethren the Rambler Classic for 1964 received a new hood and grille. A hardtop two-door was added in the top-level 770 trim, but the Classic station wagon continued to be a very popular model.

The Ambassador instrument panel for 1964 looked about the same as on the 1963 models. Note the floor shifter on this Ambassador 990-H model.

AMC president Roy Abernethy was trying to move the Ambassador further up market in 1964. Plush, exciting interiors were offered in the 990-H, as shown in this factory press photograph.

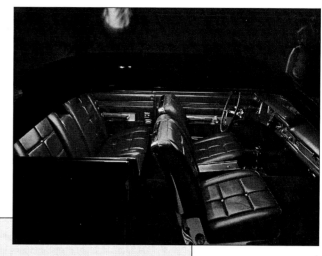

We're not exactly sure what the point of reference is supposed to be in this press release photo of the 1964 Rambler Ambassador, but it's a great picture regardless!

Rambler Ambassador wagon for 1964. In the 1964 fiscal year AMC's dollar sales were down 10 percent to just over the $1 billion mark. Profits fell to $26 million, about 30 percent lower than in 1963. Total wholesale Rambler sales worldwide fell to 455,073 units.

American Motors produced a special catalog they called the X-Ray, in which it compared its cars to other brands. Here we see some of the men who worked on the X-Ray reports. The man on the left is Carl Chakmakian; the others unfortunately are not identified.

American two-door hardtop for 1965 continued the elegant new lines that debuted in 1964, and featured a modified grille this year.

The modern 232 cid six-cylinder engine became optionally available on the 1965 American, though the 195.5 cid six offered in flathead and OHV versions remained standard equipment on most models.

Rear view of the 1965 Rambler American shows the clean, modern lines that proved so appealing to many thousands of buyers.

The neat white painted roof treatment on this 1965 Rambler American was not only stylish it was functional, since the white color kept the interior cooler in summer.

For 1965 American Motors introduced the new Rambler Marlin intermediate-sized sporty coupe. Unfortunately the public was more interested in compact sporty cars like Ford's hot new Mustang. Only 10,327 Marlins were produced that year.

Rambler Classic looked much bigger for 1965. Styling VP Dick Teague gave the Classic a wider, more prominent grille, longer rear fenders, and slab-sided bodylines. The effect was amazing—the Rambler Classic looked all new.

For the first time a sharp convertible was offered in the Rambler Classic line-up. Note that in this obviously staged photograph the girl is wearing a winter sweater and has skis, but the convertible top is down. Note, too, the lack of a background—that part would be added in later.

The big and beautiful 1965 Rambler Classic 770 wagon. A 199 cid version of the new six-cylinder became the standard engine in the Classic 550 series. All other Classics got the 232 cid six as standard.

For 1965 Rambler Ambassador got new styling that was markedly different from the lower priced Classics. A hardtop continued to be a popular Ambassador offering.

The flagship of the American Motors car line-up for 1965 was this gorgeous Ambassador convertible, the first Ambassador soft-top since 1948!

With the introduction of the restyled Classic and Ambassador all three Rambler series now offered hardtop models. Note the very dissimilar styling among the three series.

All Rambler American models were restyled for 1966. Front fenders were longer and lost their rounded shape. This American 440 convertible carried a suggested retail price of $2,486.

CHAPTER 3

AMC's Rough Ride

1966-1969

The fateful decision had been made. Beginning with the 1966 models some American Motors high-end cars would be badged as individual car lines, and not as Ramblers. The practical result was that the former Rambler Ambassador now became the 'Ambassador by American Motors,' the Rambler Marlin was now the 'Marlin by American Motors.' There is no conclusive evidence one way or the other that Roy Abernethy's ultimate intention was to eventually phase out the Rambler brand entirely. However, it was his belief that the Rambler name was tied too closely to an economy image (which, if true, was his own fault since he directed AMC sales activities prior to being made president). So initially the move to separate the top-end models from Rambler was simply to improve the big cars' sales appeal. It didn't help them very much—Ambassador sales did okay but never really hit a sustainable high level. Marlin sales, already terrible, slipped further down. And Rambler sales dropped as well.

Whether or not they fell because AMC was showing a lack of confidence in Rambler or whether it was because the company was focusing so much attention on the Ambassador line is subject to debate. But ultimately one fact remains; de-emphasizing the Rambler name did not accomplish what Abernethy had hoped for. It certainly didn't help AMC dealers.

At the announcement time for the 1966 AMC cars the big news was that Rambler American received new styling after only two years in production. The changes were obvious and attractive—the American had longer front fenders, a new hood and a new grille, the net effect of which made the American even more beautiful than before. The modern 199 cid six was now standard equipment and the 232 six could be had for a few dollars more. A 290 cid V8 became a new option, as well as a four-speed transmission. A new Rogue hardtop model debuted at the top of the line.

The Rambler Classic, which had been so thoroughly restyled for 1965, entered 1966 with only minor trim changes plus a host of new features. The 232 cid six was standard equipment, with 287 and 327 cid V8s optional. A four-speed transmission, introduced in 1965, was available with either of the V8s. A new high-end model, the two-door hardtop Rambler Rebel, was added to the Classic line-up. Classic hardtops this year featured a crisply styled new roof that was very appealing.

AMC's big sports car—the Marlin—boasted of offering "room to swing in." In sales brochures the company also declared, "You can swing to your own tempo in Marlin 66" but not many people took them up on that. Marlin production fell to just 4,547 for the model year.

The Ambassador two-door hardtop got the same crisp new roofline as the Classics, and of course the Rambler badge no longer adorned any of the Ambassadors.

Unit sales of AMC cars during the fiscal year headed downward again, dropping to just 345,886 worldwide. The company reported a net loss of $12.6 million, but the actual operating loss was much higher at almost $31 million. Tax credits helped reduce the net loss but all in all it was a very distressing year. As management noted, "There can be no minimizing the seriousness of the continuing lag in domestic

Side view of the 1966 Rambler American illustrates the more balanced lines that year. The full wheel covers, white wall tires and painted roof make this 440 model especially attractive.

automotive sales...." Rumors floated that AMC's new Chairman Roy B. Evans would soon show Roy Abernethy the door.

There was one big hope for Roy Abernethy's continuing reign. For 1967 the company would be announcing all-new big cars—the first "all-Abernethy cars," according to one magazine. These new cars were just what Abernethy said the public wanted. They were longer, wider, bigger in just about every detail, and available with a wide range of optional equipment and powerful V8 engines. Abernethy had pushed hard to get these new cars ready for a 1967 model year intro.

The styling, although an evolution of the 1965-1966 line, was much improved. Lines were smoother and more integrated. The cars looked more 'of a piece' than before. It was a sizable improvement.

The Ambassador line was particularly attractive. Ambassadors now rode a 118-inch wheelbase, two inches greater than before, so

The modern 199 cid six was now standard equipment on Americans and the 232 six could be had for a few dollars more. A 290 cid V8 was a new option, as was a four-speed transmission.

Rambler Classic for 1966 received only minor trim changes plus a host of new features. The 232 cid six was standard equipment on Classics, with 287 and 327 cid V8s optional.

bodylines stretched out over a greater length. The convertible's soft top folded completely behind the rear seat—no side panels were necessary for top storage so the rear seat was widened to hold three passengers rather than two. The Marlin was redesigned on the longer Ambassador wheelbase, creating a larger and even slower-selling sporty car.

All of AMC's mid-sized cars carried the Rambler Rebel name this year, as the Classic name was retired. Rebels were all new and rode a 114-inch wheelbase, two inches longer than before. The look was modern and mainstream, and very attractive.

As had been the case the previous year, Rambler Americans were offered in three trim series—base 220, up-level 440 and top-line Rogue. The 220 series cars were really plain with rubber floor covering and very little chrome trim. The 440 models were nicer in every detail, while the Rogue took things a step further and were rather plush. There were no significant changes in the American's looks. This was the final year for the Rambler American convertible.

The new senior cars suffered quality problems early on—perhaps because they had been rushed to market. Although the automotive press seemed to like the new Ambassador and Rebel the cars simply didn't sell very well, and that was partly

because the public had been scared off by AMC's bad financial news. Since the demise of Packard in 1958, and Studebaker in 1966, buyers had grown wary of purchasing any car that might become an orphan—and that was true even if a Big Three company produced it. DeSoto and Edsel were two good examples of that phenomenon. A recall in November 1966 of 175,000 AMC cars to fix defects

During fiscal 1966 AMC reported a net loss of $12.6 million, though the operating loss was much higher at almost $31 million. Tax credits helped reduce the net losses. AMC management noted, "There can be no minimizing the seriousness of the continuing lag in domestic automotive sales...."

AMC's big sporty car, the Marlin, didn't wear the Rambler name for 1966. In sales brochures the company declared "You can swing to your own tempo in Marlin 66" but not many people did. Marlin production fell to just 4,547 units for the model year.

Like Marlin, Ambassador dropped the Rambler name and became a separate make for 1966. Ambassador now became the 'Ambassador by American Motors.' Marlin was now the 'Marlin by American Motors.'

certainly didn't help to ease concerns. A strike by plant workers also hurt badly, coming as it did right at introduction time.

AMC had spent heavily to bring out its new big cars and within three months of introduction the company was running out of cash. Things got so bad that at one point it was apparent that the company would not be able to make its payroll at the end of the month. The board of directors finally reached their limit of patience. Roy Abernethy was dumped, replaced as president by William V. Luneburg. Roy D. Chapin, Jr., whose father was one of the founders of the Hudson Motor Car Company, took over as chairman. Chapin and Luneburg's first order of business was to secure additional bank financing to tide the company over

Flagship of the American Motors line and a very desirable collector car today—the 1966 Ambassador 990 convertible.

Ambassador and Classic two-door hardtops got a new flatter, crisper roofline for 1966, as seen here. This rare photograph was taken at a special introduction show for AMC dealers.

until a long-term solution could be worked out.

Fiscal year 1967 was a disaster for AMC. The company recorded a loss of $75 million on sales of $778 million. AMC worldwide car sales sank to just 291,090.

The big problem, as everyone could see, was a lack of faith in American Motors. Its dealers were discouraged, the automotive press was lukewarm about its products, and AMC's public image was as a loser. It was up to Roy Chapin to turn all that around.

The most important products for 1968 were two that were not likely to sell huge numbers but which would become symbols of a resurgent American Motors. The first to arrive was the Javelin, a sporty two-door pony car to compete with Mustang and Camaro. Javelin was exactly what the market called for and offered a new alternative to the Big Three pony cars. Its success was a reminder of how badly AMC had dropped the ball in 1965 by not sticking with the original Tarpon concept. Later during the 1968 model year

AMC struggled during 1967 to sell cars in the midst of negative publicity. This 1967 Rambler American carried a base price of $2,073 at introduction time but midyear was reduced to $1,839, which spurred renewed interest and increased sales.

The author's 1967 Rambler Rogue convertible. This year the American convertible became part of the Rogue line. These beauties are exceptionally rare—only 921 were produced in 1967, the final year for Rambler American convertibles.

AMC introduced its new AMX, a beautiful two-seat sports car. AMX was a revelation; after all, Ford and Chrysler didn't have a two-seater to compete with Chevy Corvette, yet little AMC did. And with its new 390 cid V8, AMX was a road burner, a real competitor. Slowly the press began to warm up to AMC once more. With the introduction of Javelin and AMX the Marlin was discontinued.

The rest of the 1968 product line was mostly carryover. Rebel was no longer badged as a Rambler. The Rebel line also saw new hardtop and convertible models in the base 550 line. The next step up for Rebel was the 770 series, and a new SST trim was the highline series. Rebel's styling was updated a bit.

Ambassadors got some refinements. The model line-up was revamped, with both the 880 and 990 series dropped. In their place was a single base Ambassador series consisting of a four-door sedan and a two-door hardtop. DPL now became Ambassador's mid-range series and included four-door sedans and station wagons plus a two-door hardtop. A new Ambassador SST series was the top-line offering and could be had in either four-door sedan or two-door hardtop styles. Sadly, the Ambassador convertible was dropped.

The only car remaining in the Rambler line was the Rambler American. It lost its convertible model but still offered two- and four-door sedans, a two-door hardtop and a popular station wagon.

AMC began to climb out of the cellar in 1968. Retail sales during the fiscal year were up 13 percent—not great but a solid improvement. Sales rebounded to $761 million and net profits were $11 million. In addition, Roy Chapin had sold the appliance division, both to raise cash and so that the company could focus on its core automotive business.

American Motors didn't have much that was really new for 1969 but it fielded several interesting variations of existing products. Both AMX and Javelin were offered in 'Big Bad' colors; Big Bad Blue, Big Bad Green and Big Bad Orange, which could be ordered at extra cost on

Rambler American wagons for 1967 were offered in two series; basic 220 and this 440 model shown. During the year AMC's board of directors made William V. Luneburg AMC's new president, and Roy D. Chapin, Jr. its chairman.

For 1967 AMC unveiled all-new big cars, intended to be just what the public wanted. They were longer, wider, bigger in just about every detail, and available with a wide range of optional equipment and powerful V8 engines.

AMC's mid-sized cars all wore the Rambler Rebel name this year, as the Classic name was retired. Rebel was completely redesigned on a 114-inch wheelbase, two inches longer than before. The look was modern and very attractive.

The last year for the Marlin was 1967. Marlin this year was built on the longer Ambassador chassis. Only 2,545 of these final-year Marlins were produced.

Ambassador styling was much improved for 1967. Lines were smoother and more integrated. Ambassadors now rode a 118-inch wheelbase, two inches greater than before, so bodylines stretched out over a greater length.

any AMC for that matter. Both of AMC's sporty car, Javelin, offered new sports options including a roof-mounted spoiler.

For 1969 Ambassador was reshaped again, with a four-inch longer wheelbase—122 inches vs. 118 inches the prior year. Ambassador's styling had an elegant new look, with a new grille and hood giving an all-new appearance. Although a single base four-door sedan continued to be offered, the real sales emphasis was put on the fancier Ambassador DPL and SST models.

Beautiful 1967 Ambassador station wagon. Fiscal year 1967 was a disaster for AMC. The company recorded a loss of $75 million on sales of $778 million. AMC worldwide car sales sank to just 291,090.

Rebels were even more attractive this year with styling refinements that included a new grille. Rebels were offered in base and SST trims levels, in two-door hardtop, four-door sedan and station wagon body styles. Now even the base two-door Rebel was a true hardtop.

The American name was dropped as AMC's entry-level car now was badged just as the 'Rambler.' Rambler continued to offer three series—base, 440 and Rogue. The base series offered two- and four-door sedans, the 440 offered four-door sedans and wagons, while the Rogue offered a single two-door hardtop model. In a surprise move the company offered a special Hurst prepared Rambler two-door hardtop dubbed the SC Rambler/Hurst, equipped with a screaming 390 cid, 315 hp V8 four-speed transmission, and a choice of two wild red/white and blue color schemes. Only 1,512 of these specialty Ramblers were produced and they are among the most collectible AMCs of all time.

AMC sales fell slightly in fiscal 1969 to $737 million and net profits dropped to $4.9 million. Worldwide wholesale unit sales of passenger cars fell slightly to 309,334. In a surprise move, management noted in its annual letter to stockholders that it had reached an agreement to purchase Kaiser Jeep Corporation. This was a

During 1968 American Motors sales efforts for the Rambler American focused on its low price and excellent value. This base American 220 series two-door had a suggested retail price of $1,946—hundreds less than a comparable Chevy Nova.

major step for the company, one that would have far reaching consequences. AMC dealers would finally have a line of trucks to offer; just as the truck market was about to enjoy tremendous growth. The acquisition of Jeep offered new opportunities for AMC to grow and expand. However, the most immediate effect would be that it would plunge the company into the red once again.

AMC finally got into the pony car market in 1968 when it introduced the new Javelin. Great styling combined with a roomy interior and a wide range of powertrain choices helped make Javelin a hit.

Midway through the 1968 model year AMC unveiled the AMX. Aside from Corvette it was the only other two-seat sports car from an American producer. AMX brought renewed admiration for AMC cars and became symbolic of the new spirit at American Motors.

Rebel dropped the Rambler brand name beginning in 1968. Because the Ambassador and Rambler Rogue convertibles had been dropped from the line the Rebel soft-top was the only AMC convertible left.

Rebel wagon for 1968. AMC began a slow recovery, with retail sales during the fiscal year up 13 percent. Sales rebounded to $761 million and net profits were $11 million.

Ambassador's model line-up was revamped for 1968. The 880 and 990 series were replaced by a single base Ambassador series consisting of a four-door sedan and a two-door hardtop. DPL became Ambassador's mid-range series and a new Ambassador SST series was the most expensive Ambassador series.

Ambassador DPL series for 1968 included four-door sedans and station wagons plus a two-door hardtop. Sadly, the Ambassador convertible was dropped.

Here are several 1968 AMC products undergoing timing runs supervised by AMC engineer Carl Chakmakian. He is seen holding a flag by the front wheel of the Rambler American.

Chakmakian waves the checkered flag during test runs of a 1968 Ambassador.

The last year for Rambler was 1969. For the final year the American name was dropped. Not surprisingly, the Rambler was still popular among buyers. A limited run of some 1,512 of these awesome 390 cid V8-powered SC Ramblers were produced during the year.

Javelin returned for 1969 featuring a new grille, new gearshift and new optional styled wheels.

AMX was the first U.S. car to feature Polyglas tires as standard equipment. AMX returned for 1969 with additional interior and exterior options including three new "Big Bad" colors: Big Bad Blue, Big Bad Green, and Big Bad Orange.

AMC Rebels were even more attractive this year with styling refinements that included a new grille. Rebels were offered in base and SST trims levels, in two-door hardtop, four-door sedan and station wagon body styles.

Ambassador was restyled again, with a four-inch longer wheelbase—122 inches versus 118 inches in 1968. Ambassador styling had an elegant look, with a new grille and hood giving an all-new appearance. Although a single base four-door sedan continued to be offered, emphasis was put on the fancier Ambassador DPL and SST models.

On April 1, 1970, American Motors introduced the first American subcompact car. Dubbed the Gremlin, it was a clever design made possible by using a shortened Hornet chassis.

CHAPTER 4

A New Look for a New Decade

1970-1975

Still working to turn AMC around, Roy Chapin and his management team settled on a program to introduce a veritable flood of new car models. The outpouring would begin with the 1970 model year introduction.

The 1970 compact cars that American Motors introduced in the fall of 1969 were of historic significance in several ways. As compacts, they replaced the previous Rambler line and in fact, marked the beginning of a new era. From that point on the Rambler brand would no longer be used in the United States (though Rambler continued to be a popular brand name in Mexico, Australia and some other countries).

The new AMC compacts bore the name Hornet, which, according to company officials, was meant to convey the idea that they were zippy, exciting and fun. Of course, the Hornet name was already owned by AMC, having been used during the 1950s on the senior Hudson cars. It cost the company about $40 million to tool up the new Hornet and the new line was meant to be a profitable volume seller. AMC's Hornet was a new idea in compact cars. As the company said, "Hornet was designed to prove that small doesn't necessarily have to mean cheap." The Hornet line-up offered a wide choice of optional equipment so buyers could tailor a car to their liking. A full range of engine choices was available including three six-cylinder engines and a V8. Ford Maverick, Hornet's closest

competitor, didn't offer anywhere near as much choice as Hornet. The AMC Hornet also rode a longer 108-inch wheelbase, two inches greater than the Rambler's. Only two body styles were offered in the Hornet line that first year, a choice of two- or four-door sedans.

Now in their third year of production, Javelin and AMX got some minor updating, including a new hood. A special red/white and blue limited edition powered by the 390 V8 was available, and also a special 'Mark Donohue' edition equipped with a spoiler carrying Donohue's signature.

AMC Rebels received several styling updates, including new rooflines for two-door models, new rear fenders, and new grilles. A special Rebel Machine model debuted, equipped with a high-performance 390 cid V8. AMC Ambassador was even better looking this year, with a new grille and new rear fenders, plus a new roofline for the two-door model.

On April 1, 1970, American Motors surprised everyone by introducing the first American subcompact car, beating both Ford and GM to the punch. Dubbed the Gremlin, it was a clever design made possible by using the Hornet as a base. Gremlin was essentially a Hornet two-door with 12 inches cut from behind the front seat. Stylists fashioned a squared-off rear end design to maximize the interior room and to give Gremlin its unique look. It was a daring design, one that

The new AMC Hornet debuted for 1970. It cost the company about $40 million to tool up the new Hornet, which replaced the former Rambler.

car buyers could not be ambivalent about. People either loved it or they hated it, but they wouldn't ignore it and that recognition was one of the goals the company was trying to achieve. The evidence was there for all to see: AMC was still in the ring, still throwing punches, still gutsy—the company that was not about to throw in the towel and give up.

Gremlin's 96-inch wheelbase didn't allow a lot of room for rear seat passengers, but then again, not too many small cars did. Gremlin's front seat room, on the other hand, was better than any other small car on the market. A 199 cid six was the standard engine, with a 232 cid six optional. Two Gremlin models were offered: a stripped two-passenger version tagged at $1,879 was the lowest

Hornet offered a wide choice of optional equipment so buyers could tailor a car to their liking. Offerings included three six-cylinder engines plus a 304 cid V8. Hornet rode a 108-inch wheelbase, two inches greater than the Rambler's. Only two body styles were offered that first year, two- and four-door sedans.

Hornet SST for 1970. AMC's Hornet was a new idea in compact cars. According to AMC, Hornet was designed to prove that small doesn't necessarily have to mean cheap.

priced American car available, while the four-passenger model was still cheap at just $1,959. The midyear introduction held down Gremlin's sales figures but demand was astounding—AMC had a real hit on its hands!

With all the news in the passenger car line it would have been easy to forget the big news on the corporate side. AMC completed the purchase of Kaiser Jeep Corporation, changed the name to simply Jeep Corporation, and put some of its best people to work refining Jeep products with an eye to reducing noise, vibration, harshness, and to improving their appeal to consumers. The cost of buying Jeep was substantial for a

AMC Javelin for 1970 showed some distinctive new styling features. Notice the raised 'power bulge' hood.

The 1970 AMX shared some of Javelin's design refinements including the pointy, power bulge hood. AMX also received a distinctive new grille this year.

struggling company like AMC and it affected the financial results for the year. Dollar volume rose substantially, to over $1 billion dollars, (a result of adding in Jeep's sales) but a loss of $56 million was recorded. Total wholesale unit sales of cars in the fiscal year was 307,334, down slightly from 1969, and Jeep sales were 93,171, down about six percent from the previous year. A high proportion of Jeep sales were to government agencies and overseas markets. U.S. consumers bought relatively few Jeeps, which was, in fact, one of Jeep's primary problems.

Although Jeep as a whole was operating profitably by the end of the fourth quarter of the year, it would be a while before the newcomer contributed very much to AMC's profits. In the

AMC Rebels got new rear styling for 1970, which is seen on the rear doors and fenders of this sharp-looking Rebel V8 sedan.

Even greater appearance changes were evident on Rebel two-door hardtops for 1970, which got heavy-looking rear quarter panels and reverse sweep 'C' pillars.

meantime, the company would have to invest money to improve Jeep's competitive position.

For 1971 AMC continued to roll out new passenger car models. In fact, 1971 may have been the busiest new car period in AMC history. An all-new Javelin debuted, larger-looking than before and boasting bulging front fenders. The two-seat AMX was dropped but a four-passenger version based on the new Javelin carried on the name and high-performance traditions of the original AMX.

Rebel was jettisoned in favor of a new nameplate—AMC Matador. The Matador in reality was just a heavily revamped Rebel, but it had very attractive new styling and rode a longer 118-inch wheelbase—the same wheelbase as the 1967/1968 Ambassador. A stylish new grille gave the car a very classy appearance. With Matador, AMC was

Continuing an effort to turn around its image with young buyers AMC offered this distinctive Rebel 'Machine' for 1970, powered by a 390 cid V8 and including a long list of standard equipment and unique features.

Stretched out on its long wheelbase, the 1970 Ambassador sedan projected a look of understated elegance.

One of the hottest AMC cars of all time—the one-year-only 1971 Hornet SC/360. Powered by a 360 cid V8 the SC/360 was a sensational performer.

Another new year—another new car! AMC introduced a completely restyled Javelin for 1971. Featuring unusual fender bulges, it created a lot of excitement among young drivers. The two-seat AMX was dropped but a sports version of the Javelin carried on the name and high-performance traditions of the original AMX.

Gremlin saw many added features for 1971 including this big folding sunroof. Gremlins equipped with this option are quite rare today and especially collectible.

Here's something you probably haven't seen before—a scene from the AMC factory. Here workers assemble part of a floor pan that is passing by on a trolley. Note the track in the factory floor.

Floor pans are clamped in fixtures prior to welding.

continuing efforts to get away from selling stripped-down base cars. Every Matador came with high-quality interior trim including full carpeting.

Hornet, all new for 1970, got two new models for 1971. The SC/360 Hornet was a sporty version, powered by a potent 360 cid V8 with a choice of two- or four-barrel carburetion. The SC/360 Hornet was good-looking and it went like hell, but the muscle car era was fast fading so it didn't sell in significant numbers. However, the other new Hornet, the Sportabout station wagon, sold like half-priced dollar bills. No other company had anything like the Sportabout. Chevy didn't even bother offering a compact station wagon, let alone one like the Sportabout, with its sporty lines and four-door utility. With Sportabout, AMC had a niche product that could sell in appreciable, solidly profitable volume.

AMC's big Ambassador got a classy new grille and continued to offer more standard equipment

This giant automatic welding unit could make up to 236 spot welds in a single operation joining the engine compartment, front and rear floor pans and a lower deck center to form underbodies for Ambassador, Matador and Javelin.

than any other car in its class. Ambassador's standard equipment included air conditioning and automatic transmission, items optional on some big cars.

Gremlin got sportier this year too. A new 'X' sports package debuted, with slotted wheels, bigger tires, bucket seat interior and bold side stripes. The base engine this year was the 232 cid six, and a new option was the 258 cid six.

The company returned to profitability during fiscal year 1971, reporting a net profit of slightly over $10 million for the year. Sales rose again, to $1.2 billion, although wholesale sales of passenger cars dropped slightly to 251,142. Jeep sales, on the other hand, rose 22.9 percent. This year the company spun off Jeep's commercial vehicles operations into a new wholly owned subsidiary called AM General. The new company would be responsible for production of military and postal vehicles, and was given a charter to identify new commercial markets to enter.

Partially completed Hornet bodies on the body production line.

Here, workers install an air duct on the assembly line. The car appears to be either a Hornet or Gremlin.

The U.S. automobile market began to take off for 1972 and AMC was ready for it. A quality improvement program yielded important gains in product quality. Although AMC had nothing really new in the way of cars, the company introduced a new warranty/customer care program called 'The Buyer Protection Plan' which was both more generous and more comprehensive than any other new car warranty. It guaranteed full coverage and promised use of a loaner car if the customer's car had to be held overnight.

Although Gremlin looked pretty much the same for 1972 it added a potent new engine option, a 304 cid V8. Hornet dropped the special SC model but offered the 360 cid V8 as a regular option. A special Gucci-designed interior was introduced on the Hornet Sportabout.

Javelin returned for 1972 sporting a very handsome new egg-crate grille. AMX, as before,

Another scene from the AMC assembly plant (circa 1971). Note Hornet cars in the background.

The former Rebel received new front-end styling for 1971 and was renamed the Matador. A longer wheelbase and increased level of standard equipment made this car an excellent value.

The Matador hardtop for 1971. The new styling was very classy. With Matador, AMC was continuing efforts to get away from selling stripped-down base cars. Every Matador came with high-quality interior trim as standard equipment.

had a fine-mesh grille with integral park/turn lamps. AMC Matador also received a new grille. In recognition of the superior performance of the AMC mid-sized automobiles the Los Angeles Police Department purchased 534 Matador police cars this year. Ambassador was further refined, with the DPL series dropped and a V8 engine now standard across the board.

Jeep vehicles came in for some real improvements this year with AMC engines integrated into all models. The old Jeep V6 engine was retired and the four-cylinder was reserved for export models only.

AMC Gremlin X, introduced for 1971, returned for 1972 looking very similar but offering several exciting new options including a V8 engine. This made Gremlin the first subcompact muscle car—and the best!

Although the Hornet SC/360 model wasn't offered this year buyers could order a 360 cid V8 on any Hornet, and turn it into a rocket! Hornet also offered an 'X' package this year, and cars so equipped are highly sought-after today.

American Motors set a new record for fiscal year sales in 1972 of $1.4 billion. Net profit was a gratifying $30 million, the best since 1964. Passenger car sales grew 20 percent to 303,000; the best level in seven years. Some 46,000 Jeep vehicles were sold. It was a very good year.

It was more of the same for 1973. Hornet got a redesigned front end and added an exciting new two-door hatchback model—an attractive innovation that drew raves from the automotive press! The Hornet line continued to offer a full range of engines including the mighty 360 cid V8. Gremlin now offered a new Levi's interior trim option that gave the look and feel of denim seats although for safety reasons the fabric was actually made of a spun nylon material. The 304

Hornet Sportabout, new for 1971, returned for 1972 with new options and new engine choices. The popularity of the Sportabout wagon was tremendous and it was a very profitable car for AMC.

The '72 American Motors Taxi

FARE-MASTER

Promise yourself the opportunity to obtain the newest of all Taxis, the 118" W.B. Matador Four Door Sedan.

Think about it . . .

- Powered by a 258 CID mileage minded 6 cyl. engine with guts (opt. 360 CID V-8).
- Backed by a heavy duty automatic trans.
- Supported by heavy duty front and rear springs, shock absorbers, and rear sway bar.
- The convenience of a side mounted rear fender gas tank filler.
- Front vent windows.
- Handling characteristics that won't quit.

Check the Matador's detailed specifications on the back page. If you were to design a Taxi, chances are you would build it like we did . . . and get the whole cab under a new Buyer Protection Plan for 12 months or 12,000 miles.

AMC kept Matador sales strong by also offering taxis and police car versions. Although most Matadors were sold to retail buyers, these fleet sales helped keep the assembly lines running smoothly and efficiently.

V8 continued to be offered and Gremlin remained the only subcompact muscle car on the market. The side stripe on the Gremlin X was different this year. Matador got a new grille, again, but other than that was mostly carryover from the previous year. Javelin and AMX were mostly carryover too, though Javelin got a noticeably different grille. Both series offered a radical new Cardin interior trim that included wild stripes on the seats and headliner.

Both Matador and Ambassador continued to offer V8 engines up to a whopping 401 cid that produced 255 hp. Ambassadors didn't get much in the way of new styling, but as in the past AMC refined and improved its biggest car to improve its appeal.

The U.S. car market was hot in 1973 and AMC made the most of it. Sales volume grew to $1.7 billion, a new record, and net profits grew

AMC Ambassador hardtop for 1972. Standard equipment on all Ambassadors was air conditioning, automatic transmission and power brakes. A rich looking new grille debuted this year.

The public loved the roominess and luxury of the Ambassador station wagon. For 1972 four V8 engines were offered in the Ambassador series.

to $85 million. Sales of passenger cars rose to a gratifying 380,000 units, while Jeep units' sales were 67,000, making Jeep a significant contributor to AMC earnings. This wasn't merely a case of a high tide raising all boats—AMC's car sales were up 25 percent versus an industry increase of eight percent.

That fall AMC introduced its first all-new car since 1971, the completely new 1974 Matador coupe. Conceived to do battle in the red-hot mid-size segment, Matador coupe offered fresh styling that included tunneled headlamps, a long hood and fastback rear styling. Offered in a range of models that even included a sporty 'X,' the Matador coupe was certainly an eye-catcher. A 'Cassini' interior trim, designed with the help of fashion expert Oleg Cassini, was a notable option. 6,165 'Cassini' Matadors were produced in 1974.

Less successfully restyled was the Matador sedan, which got a longer hood and bowed grille in an attempt to make the car look longer without spending much money. Unfortunately, it looked exactly like what it was—a minimal styling update done on the cheap. Gremlin also got a new grille this year, a year in which retail sales of Gremlins hit their all-time peak of 153,817.

Like the Matador sedan, AMC's Ambassador got a new grille and front bumper but on the Ambassador the effect was very nice, a quietly elegant look. Ambassador no longer offered a two-door model but the four-door and station wagon models continued.

Hornet saw no significant changes this year. The hot 360 cid V8 continued to be available, along

Gremlin for 1973 offered a new Levi's interior trim option that gave the look and feel of denim seats. The side stripe on the Gremlin X was different this year.

93

Hornet got restyled front-end sheet metal for 1973. The Hornet line continued to offer a full range of engines including the mighty 360 cid V8.

with the more pedestrian 232 cid and 258 cid sixes, and the 304 V8. Javelin and AMX, now in their last year of production, offered little that was new. The pony car market had shrunk drastically in the prior three years and the future didn't offer much hope for improvement. The company decided to focus its scarce development funds on other product segments.

The U.S. economy took a downward turn in 1974 as a result of a fuel crisis and the inflation that resulted from it. However, because AMC's product line was situated primarily in smaller car segments the company managed to increase its sales slightly, with 385,000 units wholesaled to U.S. dealers during the fiscal year, some 5,000

more than in 1973. Jeep sales rose eight percent to 72,000 units, and overseas sales of cars and Jeeps, including knocked down units for foreign assembly, increased to 95,794 versus 67,374 in 1973. Thus, AMC sold well over half a million vehicles this year. Dollar volume rose to just over $2 billion, a new high, although profits fell to $27 million.

Although the prior year had turned out well in spite of the poor economy, by 1975 the bad economic news was hurting everyone, AMC included. The problem was that the declining economy was triggering layoffs in many industries, and that hurt car sales. A second problem was that at the fall introduction of its 1975 line-up, AMC had almost nothing that was new.

Interestingly, Gremlin continued to offer an optional 304 V8, although since the gas crisis hit the popularity of V8s had fallen. Matador sedans and wagons got new grilles, a great improvement over the clumsy grille seen on the 1974 models. AMC trimmed its model line-up this year. Discontinued were the Javelin, AMX and Ambassador. Sales were slow and by February the company was offering rebates to try to motivate buyers.

The big reason AMC had so little new in its car line-up was that it had focused its attentions on a new small car called the Pacer, which it was bringing to market as a midyear entry. Pacer was built on a short 100-inch wheelbase, but was very wide and boasted interior dimensions equal to or greater than many mid-size cars. Its flamboyant, futuristic styling was unlike anything ever built

All AMC cars for 1973, including this Hornet four-door sedan, offered the acclaimed American Motors Buyer Protection Plan.

AMC added a beautiful hatchback model to the Hornet line for 1973. An innovative concept, the Hornet Hatchback created a great deal of interest in hatchback cars.

AMC had a great year in 1973. Sales volume grew to $1.7 billion, a new record, while net profits grew to $85 million. Sales of passenger cars rose to 380,000 units, while Jeep sales were 67,000. AMC's car sales were up 25 percent versus an industry increase of 8 percent.

before, and like Gremlin, was impossible to ignore. Introduced to the public in February and March 1975, American Motors bragged that, "When you buy any other car all you end up with is today's car. When you get a Pacer, you get a piece of tomorrow."

AMC's new Pacer came in three versions—base, sporty X and luxury D/L. Base models, beginning at $3,299, were very plain, with bench seats and base interior trim. The other Pacer models, however, were rather fancy. The X package added $339 to Pacer's price, while the D/L was $289 extra. A three-speed manual transmission was standard on all Pacers, with overdrive or automatic transmission optional.

The new Pacer was an instant hit and although it couldn't completely reverse the downward sales trend, it did help to offset some of the drop. For

Wood grain side panels and luxury wheel covers give this 1973 Hornet Sportabout a very classy image.

The Ambassador hardtop for 1973. This was the last year for the big AMC two-door. Ambassador continued to offer V8 engines up to a 401 cid that produced 255 horsepower.

Roger Moore starred as James Bond, agent 007, in the movie *The Man With The Golden Gun* in which many AMC cars were featured. Highlight of the action shots was Bond during a spiral jump over a downed bridge driving a Hornet Hatchback.

the fiscal year ending September 30, 1975, AMC reported domestic wholesale sales of 319,627 cars and 69,289 Jeep vehicles. Overseas sales of cars and Jeeps totaled more than 106,000 units. American Motors reported a loss this year of $27.5 million despite sales volume of $2.2 billion, which was more than a ten percent increase. The company announced it would soon be offering a four-cylinder engine in its passenger car line, in recognition of increasing fuel economy concerns among buyers.

What couldn't be known at this point was that the continuing effects of the fuel crisis, combined with a dramatic slow-down in demand for both Matador and Pacer, would soon plunge AMC into another crisis. Bad times were coming.

The big news for 1974 was the all-new Matador coupe, which replaced the former Matador hardtop. The coupe's styling received acclaim from many automotive writers. This sporty Matador X was an attractive model, offering sporty looks in a big family car.

There were few appearance changes in the Hornet Sportabout for 1974. The 360 cid V8 continued to be offered, along with 232 cid and 258 cid sixes and a 304 V8.

The pony car market had shrunk considerably since 1970. This would be the final year for Javelin, as AMC would focus its scarce development funds on other products.

This was also the final year for the Javelin AMX; a pity when one considers the clean, fine-looking lines of this 1974 model.

Less attractive was the grille and extended front end of the 1974 AMC Matador. The new look was an effort to make the Matador look longer and bigger.

Ambassador had been in the Nash/AMC line for more than 40 years but the 1974 model was the last of the Ambassadors. Like Matador, the Ambassador now had an extruding grille, though the Ambassador design was clean and rich looking.

AMC managed to increase its sales slightly for 1974. Some 385,000 passenger cars were wholesaled to U.S. dealers during the fiscal year, about 5,000 more than 1973. Overseas sales of cars and Jeeps increased to 95,794 versus 67,374 in 1973. Dollar volume rose to just over $2 billion. Profits fell to $27 million.

Americans saw many new safety regulations appear in the 1970s, and seat belt usage began to be emphasized as an important safety device. Here a pretty young lady demonstrates how to use the combined seat belt/shoulder harness in a 1974 Gremlin.

Four 1975 AMC models; Hornet Sportabout, Hornet two-door sedan, Gremlin X and Hornet Hatchback.

Gremlin for 1975 got new freestanding safety bumpers and other detail changes. Gremlin continued to offer an optional 304 V8, though that year the popularity of V8s had fallen due to a gas crisis.

Although Hornet continued to offer excellent value for 1975, sales were slow because of weakness in the U.S. economy. Note this well-trimmed Hornet D/L has a vinyl roof and painted wheel covers.

Hornet Hatchback for 1975. It was a difficult year for the Big Four automakers. The declining economy triggered layoffs in many industries, which hurt car sales.

Still the only four-door compact station wagon from an American producer, the Hornet Sportabout for 1975. It remained popular with families. A new 'Touring' package, shown here, included tan vinyl roof covering and back panel overlay, plus tan accents for the scuff moldings, wheel covers and grille. Inside were special seat coverings.

In 1975 AMC introduced a new small car called the Pacer as a midyear entry. Pacer was built on a short 100-inch wheelbase, but was very wide and had interior dimensions equal to many mid-size cars. Its flamboyant, futuristic styling was impossible to ignore.

This certainly was an appropriate place for American Motors to showcase the new Pacer—the National Inventors Day Exposition held in February 1975.

Pacer came in three models; base, sporty X (shown) and luxury D/L. The X package added $339 to Pacer's price, while the D/L was $289 extra. A three-speed manual transmission was standard on all Pacers, with overdrive or automatic transmission optional.

The 1975 Matador X coupe. For the fiscal year ending September 30, 1975, AMC reported domestic wholesale sales of 319,627 cars and 69,289 Jeep vehicles. Overseas sales of cars and Jeeps totaled more than 106,000 units. American Motors reported a loss this year of $27.5 million on sales volume of $2.2 billion.

After celebrating the most successful first year ever for an AMC car, sales of the AMC Pacer began to fall off rather alarmingly during 1976.

CHAPTER 5

Another Crisis

1976-1977

For 1976 Pacer continued to lead AMC's sales efforts, being its newest and most popular car. AMC's three small cars, Gremlin, Hornet and Pacer, still offered the 232 cid six as standard equipment. Matador coupes and sedans got the larger 258 cid six as standard, while the big Matador station wagon now had a 304 V8 as standard equipment. This year Gremlin was available in two models, a base Gremlin and a Gremlin Custom. The base Gremlin was a stripped price leader, while Customs had better upholstery, carpeting, custom steering wheel and a special grille. Gremlin also continued to offer the optional 304 V8, though not many were ordered; sources indicate less than 1,000 were built this year. All AMC cars this year featured solid-state electronic ignitions systems.

Pacer added a new version of the 258 cid six to the option list. Fitted with a 2bbl carburetor, this engine generated 120 hp, versus the 95 hp produced by the existing 1bbl version.

Hornet offered a wide range of appearance packages for 1976. The Sportabout wagon could be had as a basic transportation wagon, as a sporty 'X' model, as a luxury D/L, or with a special Touring interior that was both sporty and luxurious. The Hornet hatchback could be ordered plain or as a sporty 'X,' and also with the Touring interior.

Matador this year offered a plush 'Barcelona' interior and exterior trim package, which replaced the Oleg Cassini trim offered previously.

With little that was really new AMC struggled to compete in a very harsh market. Although Jeep sales remained strong, sales of passenger cars saw a sharp drop-off principally in the latter half of the model year. Even healthy profits from its AM General subsidiary couldn't offset financial losses from AMC's car division. For fiscal year 1976 the company reported a net loss of $46 million.

A crisis situation was developing. Although AMC could withstand a downturn for a certain amount of time, its slim financial resources meant it needed to return to profitability before too many more quarters passed.

For 1977 AMC gamely incorporated into its passenger car line-up as many new features as it was able to. The biggest news was the addition of a two-door station wagon to the Pacer line. Its styling seemed less flamboyant than the Pacer hatchback and the wagon sparked renewed interest in the Pacer line.

The 258 cid 1bbl six-cylinder engine was dropped and the 258 cid 2bbl was now available on Gremlin and Hornet in addition to Pacer. The 258 six remained the standard engine on Matador coupes and sedans.

Gremlin was attractively restyled with a larger rear hatchback window plus restyled, shorter front fenders and perhaps the most attractive grille ever seen on a Gremlin. New side stripes on the 'X' package also were particularly attractive. Gremlin now offered three models, a base six cylinder, a Custom six cylinder and a Custom 2.0 liter, which was equipped with AMC's new 2.0-liter four-cylinder engine. The four-cylinder had come in answer to increased fuel economy concerns among buyers but because it was costly to build management decided to offer the four only in the pricier Custom trim series.

For 1976 Gremlin continued to offer an optional 304 V8, although not many were ordered—sources indicate less than 1,000 were produced for 1976. All AMC cars this year featured solid-state electronic ignitions.

This year Gremlin was available in two models, a base Gremlin and a Gremlin Custom. The base Gremlin was a stripped price leader, while Customs had better upholstery, carpeting, and a custom steering wheel.

The Hornet line added a sporty AMX hatchback model that revived the nameplate of AMC's most famous performance car. Matador coupe had a revised Barcelona trim, which it dubbed Barcelona II.

Taken all together it just wasn't enough to reverse the downturn in AMC passenger car sales. For the fiscal year ending September 30, 1977, retail unit sales of AMC cars came to just 226,640 units—the company did not report wholesale sales to dealers this year. Jeep sales, on the other hand, rose to 117,000 units in the U.S. and Canada, a new record. The big problem was that buyer's preferences had shifted to big cars once again, while the market for domestic compact and smaller cars fell by 250,000 units. Foreign cars, too, were taking an increasing share of the U.S. car market.

However, despite the poor showing in car sales, AMC turned a small profit for 1977, because its Jeep, AM General and non-automotive businesses were all solidly profitable and able to offset losses in the passenger car area. For the year the company reported a profit of $8.2 million on sales of $2.2 billion.

That profit was simply not good enough. American Motors was operating in a very expensive industry, one that requires huge expenditures to design, develop and bring to market new products, and profits of only $8 million annually simply

Hornet Sportabout offered a wide range of appearance packages for 1976 including a sporty 'X' model, a luxury D/L, or a special Touring package.

wouldn't be enough to maintain the company as a viable business. Its car sales were going nowhere, and its Jeep and AM General business lines could carry the load only so long before they would require new investments. So the company had reached another crossroads. It needed to bring out a new car—a successful new car—and conventional wisdom was that it didn't have the money to do it.

The 1976 Hornet sedan. Although Jeep sales remained strong, sales of passenger cars saw a sharp drop-off principally in the latter half of the model year. For fiscal year 1976 the company reported a net loss of $46 million.

Hornet Hatchback for 1976. Appearance changes were kept to a minimum as the company struggled through a difficult year.

The versatility of the Hornet Hatchback was considerable and its styling was very pleasing. Note the optional vinyl top on this 1976 model.

The Matador coupe for 1976. A plush 'Barcelona' package replaced the previous 'Oleg Cassini' package.

Matador Brougham for 1976 was one of the plushiest mid-size cars on the market. Matador coupes and sedans this year got the larger 258 cid six as standard equipment.

The Matador sedan for 1976. With the demise of the Ambassador (at the end of the 1974 model year) Matador became AMC's biggest passenger car.

Matador station wagons had a 304 V8 as standard equipment. This 1976 model's wood grain panels give it a very luxurious look.

Gremlin was restyled for 1977 with a larger hatchback window plus restyled, shorter front fenders and an attractive new grille. Aggressive pricing actions led to the prices illustrated here; base model priced at $2,995 and a Gremlin Custom priced at $3,248.

This was the last year for the Hornet. This 1977 Hornet Hatchback is particularly attractive with its factory alloy wheels.

New AMC Pacers being loaded for delivery to dealers. AMC cars were shipped by rail, or by truck. Probably the best known trucking firm for AMC cars was KAT–Kenosha Auto Transport.

The biggest product news for AMC cars in 1977 was the addition of a two-door station wagon to the Pacer line. Its styling seemed less flamboyant than the Pacer hatchback and the wagon sparked renewed interest in the Pacer line.

Advertising for the new Pacer wagon was aimed at younger families and women in particular. The new station wagon attracted many young families.

A view taken inside the American Motors body plant where a 1977 Pacer wagon body is being welded together by ultra-modern automatic welding equipment.

The 258 cid six remained the standard engine on Matador coupes and sedans for 1977. Appearance-wise there was little new on the Matador sedan.

Matador wagon for 1977. Despite poor car sales, AMC turned a small profit for 1977, because Jeep, AM General and AMC's non-automotive businesses were profitable enough to offset losses in the passenger car area. For the year the company reported a profit of $8.2 million on sales of $2.2 billion.

113

As a young AMC salesman in Connecticut the author had a 1978 AMX demonstrator identical to the one shown here. AMX this year was produced on the Concord Hatchback body, similar to the Hornet AMX that had appeared in 1977.

CHAPTER 6

Revival and Reward

1978-1979

Lacking the enormous sums of money neccessary to design a whole new line of cars AMC was left with very few choices. Certain very senior members in management had argued that the company should cease car production entirely and concentrate the bulk of its resources on Jeep. That legendary line of four-wheel-drive vehicles was tremendously popular and very profitable. Jeep, combined with the other businesses owned by AMC—namely Wheel Horse lawn equipment, AM General Corporation, plus an assortment of component suppliers—would make a non-car-producing American Motors Corporation a vastly profitable concern.

But others argued that producing automobiles provided a necessary balance to the company's operations, and if another gas crisis appeared Jeep sales might decline while car sales might go up. Besides, for more than 75 years the company had been primarily an automobile manufacturer; building automobiles was its heritage and to cease producing cars was simply unthinkable.

However, all the discussions could not alter one inescapable fact; in order to continue as an automobile manufacturer the company needed a viable new car to sell. And like the U.S. Cavalry coming to the rescue just in the nick of time, the styling department at AMC came up with a sharp new car dubbed the Concord D/L that would save the company, at least for a time.

Concord was AMC's entry into the "luxury compact" field pioneered by Ford Granada. With Concord D/L, buyers got an American-size compact with the sort of luxury features usually found in larger, more expensive cars, things like a quartz digital clock, wood grain instrument panel,

individual reclining seats with plush fabrics and Mercedes-like painted wheel covers. Two-door D/Ls came with a landau-style vinyl with 'opera windows'—easily the most desirable styling touch of the 1970s. Concord D/L also included extra quiet insulation, which with Concord's revised suspension, combined to provide a quiet, soothing driving experience.

The base Concord line this year, consisting of two- and four-door sedans, a station wagon and a two-door hatchback, was actually not much different than the old Hornet, but AMC cleverly priced the D/L option package at a low $299. Nearly everyone opted to pay the extra money to get the greater value it represented. A Sport package that included bucket seats and slot-styled wheels was also offered on all models but apparently not many were ordered.

The AMC Concord was perhaps the cleverest bit of restyling since the 1961 Rambler. The Concord wasn't really new; it was a restyled AMC Hornet. And not much had been redone—the shorter front fenders were new, as was the hood, the rear fenders were somewhat reshaped and the tail lamps were new. If these changes had been done simply to update the Hornet's styling, the program most likely would have failed.

But Concord was more than the sum of its parts—it really seemed to be an all-new car. The level of luxury it provided was above par for the times and quite unexpected, but very appreciated. Buyers flocked to AMC stores.

Since there was no Hornet this year, there was no Hornet AMX. But AMC wisely decided to continue offering an AMX model, using the Concord/Hornet hatchback body matched with

Introduced for 1978, Concord D/L was AMC's entry into the 'luxury compact' field. With Concord, buyers got an American-size compact with luxury features usually found in larger, more expensive cars.

the new style front fenders and a very attractive new grille.

AMC's Gremlin X got redesigned stripes again this year, and a one-year-only Gremlin GT model was produced, probably the rarest and most collectible Gremlin of all. Pacer was also restyled, with a raised grille and new hood greatly altering the aerodynamic styling of the front end. Lastly, the Matador line returned with only minimal changes, chief of which was the availability of the Barcelona Package on the Matador sedan.

During the year American Motors took some major steps to improve its financial results. Automobile production was consolidated to one plant in Kenosha, Wisconsin. The old Milwaukee

Concord D/L two-door featured a vinyl half-top with side 'opera windows.' Regardless of how one feels about such features today, in 1978 they were considered the very height of fashion and taste.

In 1978, its final year in production in the U.S., Gremlin offered little that was new. Interestingly, the popular Gremlin nameplate continued in Mexico several years after it ceased being used in America.

116

Pacer hatchback sales were slow again in 1978, as the novelty of its design was no longer drawing the crowds it once had. All Pacers for 1978 received new front-end styling.

Pacer station wagons were still popular; their more conventional looks and greater carrying capacity appealed to young suburban families.

The AMC Matador line returned with only minimal changes, chief of which was the availability of the Barcelona Package on the Matador sedan.

body plant was converted to component manufacturing and the Brampton, Ontario, Canada plant was converted to production of Jeep CJ vehicles. The company also phased out its standard transit bus business so that AM General could focus on more profitable lines.

These moves, along with very gratifying sales of Concords and Jeep vehicles, turned the tide for AMC—sales for the fiscal year rose to $2.5 billion and net profits climbed to $36 million. Wholesale sales of passenger cars worldwide fell slightly to 214,537, of which 193,803 were in the U.S. and Canada. Jeep unit sales grew to 180,667 worldwide. With the company moving in the right direction it would only take a good economy to get it back to full health.

1978 Matador wagon. AMC's sales for the 1978 fiscal year rose to $2.5 billion and net profits climbed to $36 million. Wholesale sales of passenger cars worldwide fell slightly to 214,537, of which 193,803 were in the U.S. and Canada.

In 1979 AMC rolled out another new car, the Spirit. Though based on the former Gremlin, Spirit Liftback's styling was much sportier.

AMC's new chairman, Gerry Meyers, believed that long term AMC would need to have a partner to help it develop new passenger car models. AMC could get along for the short term with redesigns of its existing products but over the long haul it needed the sort of highly fuel-efficient cars that Europe and Japan had. The advanced designs necessary to compete in the 1980s would require completely redesigned products—right down to smaller, lighter door handles, was the way one prominent executive put it. Such an effort was probably more than AMC would be able to afford, so Meyers wanted to explore the possibility of acquiring the needed designs from another manufacturer. A deal was discussed with Peugeot in which AMC would take over distribution of

A simple yet very elegant grille and attractive fastback styling marked the new-for-1979 AMC Spirit Liftback.

Also appearing for 1979 was the new Spirit Sedan, which bore a closer resemblance to the former Gremlin. Spirit Sedans were badged as Germlins in Mexico.

Peugeot cars in America, with a goal of eventually producing Peugeot-based cars in the Wisconsin plant. But almost at the last moment Renault asked if they could be allowed to submit a proposal for essentially the same arrangement. Meyers agreed, and before long both French automakers were competing for the deal.

A confident American Motors entered the 1979 model year with another new car to unveil—the subcompact AMC Spirit. Like Concord, Spirit was not completely new but was a major revision of an existing platform, in this case the AMC Gremlin. But although the Spirit sedan model used the basic Gremlin body, the two-door Spirit Liftback, volume seller in the Spirit line, had a new body style with low, sporty lines. It utilized the Gremlin/Spirit sedan floor pan, cowl, front fenders, hood and more, but had a fastback roof for a more youthful look.

The Spirit was offered in a base series, as well as up-level D/L and top-line Limited versions. In addition, Spirit Liftback could be ordered with a GT package that included spoke-styled wheels, radial tires, sports steering wheel, sport outside mirror, and special instrumentation.

AMX returned this year in a new guise. Built on the new Spirit Liftback body, AMX was smaller and sportier than before—in fact, almost the size of the original 1968 version! Powered by a standard 258 cid six-cylinder engine, AMX also offered an optional 304 cid V8 for performance more matching its heritage.

Concord, the AMC success story of 1978, returned with a new grille and new wheel covers.

For the third year in a row there was a redesigned AMX. Based on the new Spirit Liftback body this was a surprisingly good variation of the AMX theme. Offering a choice of the 258 cid six or 304 cid V8, this AMX reflected the era it was produced in.

The Concord line-up was now formally split into three distinct series. Concord base came with a bench seat, plain chrome wheel covers, and standard trim, while Concord D/L came with a host of luxury items, and Concord Limited took the level of luxury to a new height with its standard leather seats. Concord D/L two-doors came with the landau-style vinyl roof as before, but the four-door D/L had a new vinyl half-roof.

The AMC Pacer returned to the line with little that was really new, though like the other lines Pacer now offered a Limited model with genuine leather interior.

The AMC Matador was noticeably absent from the line-up—it had been dropped due to slow sales and the need to trim automobile production costs.

Early in the calendar year the company announced that it had reached an agreement with Renault of France. Within a few months time, AMC said, its dealers would begin selling Renault LeCar mini-cars. These highly fuel-efficient midgets would give dealers a product to compete with the Japanese makes that were grabbing an increasing share of the small car market. Future benefits of the AMC/Renault agreement would include having AMC dealers sell the larger Renault 18i, while Renault dealers would sell Jeeps in certain overseas markets. Eventually the company would produce a Renault-designed car in its Wisconsin plant.

AMC had a very good year during fiscal 1979. Worldwide wholesale car sales fell again to 207,557 of which 184,456 were sold in the U.S.

Concord for 1979 got a handsome new grille and a number of improvements. Concord sales continued to be strong in this, its second year.

and Canada, but Jeep sales climbed to 175,647 in the U.S. and Canada, 207,642 worldwide, marking the first year that Jeeps outsold cars. Dollar volume rose to $3.1 billion, a record, and net profits grew to $83.9 million.

What wasn't generally known was that AMC had just enjoyed the last really good year it would ever have. Another fuel crisis had emerged, triggering rampant inflation, high unemployment and record high interest rates. Its early effects were seen in Jeep sales, which slowed down midway through the year. Although Jeep's momentum had been strong enough to end up the fiscal year with record sales, the four-wheel-drive market was fast running out of steam and when it did Jeep and AMC's future would be in danger. The final crisis was at hand.

Along with the new grille Concord four-door sedans also got a new half vinyl top this year. The Concord line-up was now formally split into three distinct series; base, D/L and Limited.

One of the more popular Concord models was the station wagon, especially in upscale D/L or Limited trim.

Although AMC continued to offer a Concord Hatchback, few were sold. Advertising and marketing emphasis again was mainly on the two- and four-door sedans.

The AMC Pacer returned to the line with little that was really new, though like the other lines Pacer now offered a Limited model with genuine leather interior.

Pacer wagon for 1979. During fiscal 1979 AMC's worldwide wholesale car sales fell to 207,557 of which 184,456 were sold in the U.S. and Canada. Jeep sales climbed to 175,647 in the U.S. and Canada, 207,642 worldwide, marking the first year that Jeeps outsold cars. Dollar volume rose to a record $3.1 billion. Net profit was $83.9 million.

Spirit GT Liftback for 1980. A new four-cylinder engine debuted for 1980, the 2.5-liter 'Iron Duke' produced by GM. To cut costs AMC sold the Richmond, Indiana plant where its 2.0-liter four was built and contracted with GM for the engines it would need.

CHAPTER 7

The Final Decade

1980-1987

The first year of the final decade in which American Motors would still be a part of the automotive industry should have been a great one for the company. No less an expert than Bob Irvin of the industry trade paper *Automotive News* declared that the "AMC comeback looks real." After all, early in the year the one-millionth Jeep produced by AMC rolled off the assembly line in Toledo, Ohio. The popular Concord was entering its third year with a host of innovations; AMC Spirit was in only its second year on the market and best of all, AMC was introducing another whole new range of premium-priced automobiles. The prior year had been a great one for AMC.

A new four-cylinder engine debuted for 1980, the 2.5-liter 'Iron Duke' produced by GM. Wishing to save the considerable expense of building its own four, AMC sold the Richmond, Indiana plant where its 2.0-liter four was built and contracted with GM for the engines it would need. The 2.5-liter was by then a better choice for AMC, since it was gutsy enough to be used in Jeep CJs, where it was needed to improve Jeep's fuel economy.

The new four became the standard engine for both Spirit and Concord. Although a few four-cylinder Pacer test cars had been built, the results were under-whelming and it was clear that a four-cylinder engine wasn't going to revive Pacer's stagnant sales. Only one six-cylinder engine was offered in AMC cars this year, the trusty 258 cid in-line six with 2bbl carburetor. A four-speed transmission became standard equipment across the board to optimize fuel economy. In line with decreased demand brought about by the fuel crisis

as well as a need to meet federal fuel economy regulations AMC discontinued offering V8 engines in its passenger cars this year.

Concord continued its successful three-series line-up this year, offering base, D/L and Limited models. All Concords sported a new horizontal grille and wraparound tail lamps, while the D/L and Limited also included a new vinyl roof covering and attractive new opera windows. Two- and four-door sedans and a station wagon were offered—the slow-selling Concord Hatchback was discontinued. Concord no longer offered body-color wheel covers but had sporty argent styled plastic wheel covers as standard equipment on the D/L series. Chrome wheel discs were standard on base models while the Limited now included wire wheel covers.

Spirit also continued with a three-series strategy, offering its Liftback and Sedan models in a choice of base, D/L or Limited trim. The popular GT package continued to be offered as an option. AMX also continued as a separate model but because the V8 engine had been dropped this year AMX had the 258 cid six as its sole engine offering. AMC's Pacer, now in its final year, was available in hatchback or wagon form in either D/L or Limited trim.

The big news for 1980 was another new AMC car line—the third new offering in as many years. The new series was the Eagle, the first four-wheel-drive passenger car from an American producer. Eagle mated the body of AMC's Concord with rugged four-wheel-drive components to produce a car that offered comfort and luxury along with

Spirit for 1980 continued with a three-series strategy by offering Liftback and Sedan models in a choice of base, D/L or Limited trim. The 2.5-liter four became the standard engine for both Spirit and Concord.

go-anywhere capability. The Eagle line included the same three body types as Concord—two- and four-door sedans plus a four-door station wagon. However, Eagle was offered only in two high-line trim levels, base and Limited, with the base Eagle equivalent to a Concord D/L. No stripped-down models or base-level trims were offered. In addition, Eagle came with only one powertrain,

The Spirit Sedan models, with slightly more room than the Liftback, plus a lower price, offered excellent value.

the 258 cid six with automatic transmission and fully automatic full-time four-wheel-drive. Eagle's independent front suspension was unique and a distinct product advantage.

Because it was raised a few inches on its chassis AMC's Eagle was a bit unusual looking at first glance. One magazine said it looked like a Concord standing on its tiptoes. But Eagle's bad weather and off-road performance were absolutely astounding! Even the harshest critics of AMC products were won over to Eagles' standard once they drove one through an off-road course. Yet Eagle was intended mainly as an on-road vehicle that provided safe, secure driving in the worst conditions. Reports indicated that roughly 40 percent of early buyers were women.

Eagle was a smart move. Because it shared the same body shell and most of the interior fittings of the Concord, it could be produced in the same plant. Relatively little tooling expense was incurred, and Eagle used essentially the same six-cylinder engine as the other cars. Equally important, the people who were buying Eagles were mostly newcomers to the AMC line. Some were owners of big SUVs looking to downsize but most buyers were people who understood the advantages of four-wheel-drive SUVs but desired those benefits in a more car-like conveyance.

This was the final year for the AMC Pacer. Several thousand of 1980 models were built before production ended in December 1979.

Another product highlight of the busy 1980 model year was the introduction of a factory Ziebart rust protection program on all AMC cars. This was a factory-engineered system in which critical areas of bodies were given a coating of Ziebart during assembly, but it also relied heavily on galvanized body panels, wax coatings in closed body cavities, plus plastic inner fender liners. Some buyers mistakenly thought the cars were simply treated to the standard Ziebart aftermarket undercoating and rust proofing but the actual factory process was much more comprehensive. In an era when most cars lacked even basic factory rust proofing it was not uncommon to see three- or four-year-old cars with rust-through, so the AMC cars had a clear product advantage.

Of course, many AMC dealers also had Renault cars to sell this year and they were selling at a pretty good clip. Jeep sales, on the other hand, were not. Total 1980 model year production for Jeep fell by more than half.

The results of the drastic fall-off in Jeep sales could be seen in the pages of American Motors' annual report for 1980. AMC made a fundamental change in its financial reporting this year, going to a fiscal year that ran January 1 through December 31, so the annual report was now based on the calendar year. In prior years the fiscal year ended on September 30, roughly equivalent to the industry's model year.

During calendar year 1980 American Motors lost $197.5 million, an astronomical figure, one which to financial analysts must have seemed almost beyond belief. Net sales fell to $2.5 billion versus $3.2 billion in calendar year 1979. Unit sales of cars in the U.S. and Canada were steady at 203,251 during the calendar year, plus another

Pacer models for 1980 were offered in either D/L or Limited trim. Although several four-cylinder Pacers were built for testing, they never reached production.

The AMC Concord D/L for 1980. Concord continued its successful three-model line-up this year: base, D/L and Limited.

25,686 in international markets. But a decline in Jeep sales of some 90,000 units put the firm deep in the red. The new decade had begun in upheaval and would remain that way for some time.

Luckily, product plans for 1981 had long been set so when the 1981 line-up debuted AMC had some new cars to show off. Big news was that the Eagle line got two new models, the Eagle Kammback and the Eagle SX/4. Both were based on the AMC Spirit, the Kammback using the Spirit sedan (nee Gremlin) body, while the SX/4 used

To keep its popular Concord fresh and appealing, AMC introduced a new vinyl top and revised opera windows for the two-door D/L this year. All Concords this year sported a new horizontal grille and wraparound tail lamps.

the Spirit Liftback body shell. Unlike the larger Eagles the new smaller Eagles came in base and D/L trims that were equivalent to their Spirit counterparts. In addition, a Sport package for the SX/4 was similar to the Spirit GT package. A Sport package was also offered, with some equipment differences, on the senior Eagle two-door sedan and station wagon, though curiously not on the Eagle four-door sedans.

Spirit and Concord got only detail changes this year. As was the case with Eagle, all exterior sheet metal was now one-sided galvanized steel. The Limited series was dropped from the Spirit line—with inflation raising car prices at a furious clip the extra expense for the Limited apparently was too much for most buyers.

Another new car line being offered by AMC dealers for 1981 was the Renault 18i compact four-door sedans and wagons in roughly the same size category as a Concord but offering a European flavor. The 18i was heavily promoted by AMC and the company believed it would sell in large numbers but for some reason buyers didn't warm up to it. Sales of the 18i were embarrassingly low.

The U.S. economy was in terrible shape again this year. Two and one-half years of a devastated economy had enacted a toll on many U.S.

Concord D/L and Limited four-door sedans for 1980 got a restyled roof with very handsome quarter windows. Base Concord sedans continued to use the old Hornet style roof panel.

companies and AMC was one of them. Running out of cash, AMC was forced to accept an equity buy-in by Renault, in which the French automaker eventually ended up owning more than 40 percent of the U.S. firm. The continuing slump in Jeep sales was the cause; it kicked the legs out from under any plan of revival.

The best financial news AMC could report that awful year was that the company had lost 'only' another $136 million—this after the $200 million loss it had experienced the prior year. Car sales in the U.S. and Canada declined to 179,834 units during fiscal year 1981, while climbing slightly in overseas markets to 26,907. Jeep sales grew in

Concord D/L and Limited wagons for 1980 had a thick new molding on the rear side windows, a styling trick to make the window area look larger. There were quality issues with this item and some 1980 D/L models were produced without it.

AMC introduced another new product in 1980, the extraordinary Eagle four-wheel-drive automobiles. Using the Concord body with a single speed four-wheel-drive transfer case, Eagle was the first American car to offer the safety of all-wheel-drive.

The lowest priced model in the new Eagle line was this two-door Eagle sedan. The trim was equivalent to the Concord D/L series, though Eagle didn't wear D/L nameplates.

Oh, to have one of these today! AMC Eagle is supremely capable in all kinds of weather and on all types of road surfaces.

overseas markets but fell again in the U.S. and Canada. AMC's chairman, Gerry Meyers, was shown the exit, replaced at the helm by W. Paul Tippett.

Behind the scenes American Motors was scrambling to design new products to save the company. The first one out of the gate would be a new Renault-based small sedan to resurrect the passenger car division, followed by a new Cherokee to turn Jeep around. But new products take time to develop and bring to market; for 1982 AMC would have to rely on warmed over versions of its existing vehicles.

Because fuel economy was still a vital product advantage in the minds of most buyers AMC's five-speed manual transmission was a very welcome new feature. Offered as an option on all 1982 AMC cars and most Jeep vehicles, the new five-speed offered greatly improved gas mileage. With the standard four-cylinder engine and optional five-

For 1981 all AMC passenger cars featured one-sided galvanized steel for all exterior body panels. The Spirit sedan in D/L trim was a very attractive automobile.

Spirit Liftback for 1981 looked almost identical to prior years but offered many improvements. The author was an AMC salesman back then and drove a bright red Liftback demo car with a side stripe like that shown here.

Concord D/L and Limited models continued to offer superior value and reliability in the luxury compact class.

speed the highway gas mileage rating for Concord and Spirit was an incredible 37 mpg.

Spirit and Concord got one new interior color (slate blue) and seven new exterior colors but other than that had little that was new appearance-wise. A new wide-ratio automatic transmission offering improved fuel economy with no loss in performance was optional with the six-cylinder engine.

Eagles now included the Select Drive four-wheel-drive system as standard equipment. Select Drive, introduced as an option midway through the 1981 model year, allowed a driver to switch from four-wheel drive to two-wheel drive for improved fuel economy. The driver could do this without leaving the vehicle; moving a lever on the instrument panel made the change. All

Eagles now came standard with the 2.5-liter four-cylinder engine.

With not much new product-wise, and saddled with extremely high development costs for new car and Jeep models, there was little hope that AMC could turn a profit in 1982. A continuing poor economy made it virtually impossible. Although sales rose to $2.8 billion the company reported a loss of $153 million—its third giant loss in as many years. But the good news was that its first all-new car in years was ready to be introduced.

The new car, dubbed the Renault Alliance, was based on the recently introduced European Renault R-9. The basic design was upgraded to appeal to American tastes with redesigned interior trim, a richer looking grille, a more powerful fuel-injected engine, and a broader array of optional equipment. It was aimed at a large market segment; small family sedans below intermediate size. Though officially in the subcompact segment, Alliance offered so much interior room for its size that the EPA classified it a compact car. Officially Alliance was a Renault-brand product, but it also carried the AMC name on the back. For European markets the Renault was offered only as a four-door sedan, but for the U.S. market AMC stylists designed a sharp-looking two-door sedan. Renault Alliance offered a range of models in base, L, D/L and Limited series. Pricing was excellent, with the basic two-door offering a starting price of just $5,595. Although that was higher than some old-

Concord D/L sedan for 1981. Although a four-cylinder engine was standard equipment on Concord most buyers ordered the 258 six-cylinder instead. It was smoother, quieter, much more powerful and yet it still provided excellent gas mileage.

style small cars still on the market, for a modern, roomy sedan with front-wheel drive, fuel injection, excellent ride and superior handling qualities it was an outstanding price. Alliance provided room for five passengers, whereas the competition offered only four-passenger models. Alliance also provided exceptional fuel economy—an EPA rating of 37 mpg in city driving and 52 mpg on the highway. Best of all, Alliance was an exceptionally attractive small car, more stylish and modern than just about any other small car.

The Alliance was a hit, the most successful new product launch in the company's history. *Motor*

A quick glance reveals one of the new features of the 1981 Eagle—a bold new grille. Note the optional alloy wheels on this two-door model.

A 1981 Eagle four-door sedan wearing the standard plastic wheel covers. Like other AMC cars, the Eagles used galvanized steel for all exterior body panels, which is one reason why so many have survived, even in harsh climates.

Trend magazine named it 'Car of the Year,' which was the first time an AMC-produced car had won that awarded that since 1963.

The company also offered its carryover Spirit and Concord, though it announced early in the year that 1983 would be the final year for both. AMC's six-cylinder engine became standard

New this year was Select Drive, in which the driver could switch from four-wheel-drive to two-wheel-drive at the flick of a switch.

equipment on both series, and the four-cylinder was not available this year for either model. Concord was offered only in four-door sedan and wagon models; the two-door had been dropped. Concord four-door models were available in base and D/L trim, while the wagon was offered in D/L and Limited models.

The Spirit sedan was axed; in fact it had been dropped midway through the 1982 model year. The handsome Spirit Liftback didn't offer a base model this year. However, a new model joined the carryover D/L. It was dubbed the Spirit GT and it was very similar to the GT package offered in previous years. The big difference was that this year it wasn't an option package but a separate model—really the last new model introduced to carry the AMC brand name. With the standard 258 cid six, tachometer, sports steering wheel, aluminum wheels, fog lamps, handling package, steel-belted radial tires, and sporty exterior trim, it was a great machine.

The company's line of Eagle automobiles received few changes for 1983. Some of what little attention it got was negative; the Eagle Kammback was dropped, and also the senior Eagle two-door sedan. The SX/4 this year was offered in base, D/L and Sport versions, the Eagle four-door sedan was

American Motors continued to roll out new products with the introduction of the 1981 Eagle Kammback. Based on the Spirit sedan body its low price of $5,995 made it an outstanding value.

The hot new AMC product for 1981 was the new Eagle SX/4, which used the Spirit Liftback body to produce a four-wheel-drive sporty car. There was nothing else like it anywhere and these models sold well considering the tough economic environment they had to contend with.

Most popular of all the Eagle models was, perhaps surprisingly, the most expensive—the Eagle station wagon. Good looks, safety and versatility were just some of its many attributes.

AMC dealers had the Renault LeCar to offer again in 1981. Two-and-a-half years of a devastated economy had enacted a toll on AMC. Running out of cash it was forced to accept an equity buy-in by Renault, in which the French automaker eventually ended up with effective control of the U.S. firm.

Another new car offered by AMC dealers in 1981 was the Renault 18i compact four-door sedans and wagons. The 18i's were heavily promoted by AMC and the company believed they would sell in large numbers, but buyers didn't warm up to the product. Sales of the 18i were embarrassingly low.

offered only in one trim level, equivalent to a D/L, while the wagon offered that trim plus Limited and Sport versions. The four-cylinder engine remained standard equipment. A new 2:73 'performance' axle ratio was offered on six-cylinder Eagles with automatic transmissions. The six offered higher compression.

Because of slow sales the Renault import line had to be thinned a bit. Before the summer was over the company announced it was dropping the Renault LeCar from its line-up, along with the 18i sedan. The 18i wagon would continue to be offered but would be renamed the Renault Sport Wagon.

A news article appeared in an industry trade paper during February 1983. It stated that AMC would replace its Eagles with a new Renault Alliance-based product for 1985. That sounded

With fuel economy an increasingly important feature AMC's five-speed manual transmission was a welcomed new option. Offered on all 1982 AMC cars and most Jeep vehicles, the new five-speed offered greatly improved gas mileage. With the standard four-cylinder engine and optional five-speed the highway gas mileage rating for Concord and Spirit was an incredible 37 mpg.

Spirit GT Liftback for 1982. A new wide-ratio automatic transmission offering improved fuel economy with no loss in performance was optional on AMC cars with the six-cylinder engine.

1982 Spirit D/L Liftback. Although AMC's sales rose to $2.8 billion the company reported a loss of $153 million—its third giant loss in as many years.

like good news, since it implied that the company intended to continue producing the Eagle line.

It was a year filled with mixed emotions. Car sales climbed to their highest level in seven years, over 270,000 worldwide, but most of those were the new Renault products. Indeed, with AMC's expertise Renault set a new record for sales in the U.S. with 179,419 compared to the old record of 91,981 set in 1958. Jeep vehicles rose too, but not nearly so high. During 1983 the company reached an agreement to assemble Jeep vehicles

in China—the first American company to do so in the modern era.

Sales volume during 1983 was $3.2 billion, up considerably from the two prior years. But although the company reported a modest profit in the fourth quarter, for the full year AMC reported a net loss of $258 million.

For 1984 AMC introduced perhaps the most important new products of the decade, the all-new Jeep Cherokee and Wagoneer XJ. These downsized Jeep wagons were AMC's best hope to

Concord wagon for 1982. The optional spoke wheels are a nice touch.

stem the losses that had plagued the company for too long.

On the car side of the firm there was a new Renault Encore, a hatchback version of the Alliance. Offered in two- and four-door models, the Encore was a nice package but with the market rapidly moving back to larger cars AMC didn't really need to be introducing another subcompact car; it needed help in the mid-size category. Alliance got detail changes, including removal of the chrome AMC nameplate on the back. However, to appease longtime AMC buyers an AMC logo sticker was placed in the rear window.

With Concord and Spirit gone the only real AMC brand cars for 1984 were the Eagles. The four-cylinder engine was once again standard equipment. Fuel economy ratings for the four-cylinder/four-speed combo were 24-mpg city, 30-mpg highway. The five-speed was rated the same for city driving but achieved a rating of 32 mpg for highway driving. Eagle prices were $9,495 for the four-door sedan, $10,225 for the regular station wagon, and $10,695 for the Eagle Limited wagon. The Eagle SX-4 was dropped.

There was some interesting future product news. The company reported that it would begin importing the high-performance Renault Alpine sports car in the summer of 1986, as well as the Renault Espace minivan.

In addition, the company announced it had purchased 250 acres of land in Brampton, Ontario, Canada on which it would construct a new automobile assembly plant. In that plant the company would produce an all-new intermediate-size car it was intending to introduce for 1987.

For 1984 the company saw a dramatic increase in sales. The total for the year was $4.2 billion—up nearly $1 billion from the year before. The company managed a profit for the full year but it was perilously thin at just $15 million. It was the first full-year profit AMC had reported since 1979. Unbelievably, wholesale car sales during the fiscal year actually fell about 28,000 units despite Alliance being in only its second year on the market and in spite of the introduction of the new Encore. Jeep sales rose almost 80,000 units and sales of AMC cars and Jeep vehicles rose in international markets, so overall the company could report an increase in total vehicle sales of about 59,000 units.

But the next year things got bad again. What looked at first to be the turnaround that everyone

For 1982 AMC highlighted two-tone paint on the Concord D/L and Limited two-doors. With wire wheel covers and two-tone paint this Concord Limited has a look of luxury and style.

139

Concord D/L four-door sedan. As attractive as the AMC cars were, the worldwide economic downturn kept sales below a profitable level.

1982 SX/4 D/L model. Eagles now included the Select Drive four-wheel drive system as standard equipment. Select Drive, introduced as an option midway through the 1981 model year, allowed a driver to switch from four-wheel-drive to two-wheel drive for improved fuel economy.

This is a 1982 Eagle SX/4 with the optional Sport package. All Eagles now came with the 2.5-liter four-cylinder engine standard.

Eagle Kammback for 1982 was a great little car that unfortunately didn't receive the marketing support it deserved, so unit sales were never very high.

The alloy wheels on this Kammback give it a decidedly sporty appearance, almost like a mini-Cherokee.

Although Eagle's four-wheel drive system lacked a low range the car was perfectly capable of light-duty off-road use.

was hoping for proved to be illusory. Instead of experiencing a continuing upward climb during the 1985 fiscal year, American Motors got hammered. The company reported a net loss for the year of $125 million on sales of just over $4 billion. Cars, once again, were the problem, for although Jeep sales in the U.S. and Canada rose by 46,000 units, wholesale sales of passenger cars fell by 100,000. Inversely, sales of AMC cars in overseas markets continued to grow, reaching 14,492, up 10,000 units from two years previously.

The 1985 AMC car line-up suffered from having too little that was new. The Alliance, although a nice car, was struggling against better-known competitors in a market segment that was rapidly shrinking. Encore had flat-out failed. Encore offered essentially the same package as the Alliance but its styling didn't appeal to American tastes. Although it offered an attractively priced base model, its up-level models were priced almost the same as the Alliance. A new convertible was offered in the Alliance line, but with a sales goal of 7,000 units

For 1982 the Eagle wagon continued to be the most popular of the Eagle models.

it wouldn't make much of a difference in company fortunes one way or another.

The Eagle line was shrunk down to just the four-door sedan in a single base model and the wagon in base and Limited models and that was it. The six-cylinder engine was made standard equipment; the five-speed was also standard, so the only powertrain option now was the popular automatic transmission. Eagle got some minor appearance changes; new wheel covers plus the hood/grille combo formerly used on Eagle SX/4.

There was some good news. The new joint venture in China began production of Jeep Cherokees, a new Comanche pick-up was introduced in the U.S. and Jeep sales set a new record of 240,288 units worldwide.

Eagle wagon with the optional Sport package for 1982. A surprising number of these were sold. The sporty looks and four-wheel-drive capability were a combination that appealed to many families.

Eagle's ability to go in the snow was remarkable. The smoothness and ease of use of its full-time four-wheel-drive system made it a viable alternative to big, heavy SUVs.

For 1983 the Spirit GT became a model rather than an option package, and was the last new AMC-branded model to be introduced. With a long list of standard features it created renewed interest in the Spirit, to the surprise of the company and its dealers.

The year 1983 was the last for both the Concord D/L and the Spirit. Hereafter AMC would offer only Eagle and Renault cars plus Jeep vehicles.

But time was running out for AMC. The company was working at a frantic pace to design an all-new intermediate-size car, because that was now the hottest segment of the market. The French owners of the company had not yet learned to anticipate the U.S. market and were once again trying to catch up with changing trends. Although it would be a completely new design, built in North America and not based on an existing Renault, the new intermediate car would be badged as a Renault. Meanwhile the AMC brand name continued to suffer from willful neglect.

For 1986 the AMC Eagle returned and again any changes and improvements were minimal. Essentially the identical models and options from

AMC Eagle got few changes for 1983. Eagle Kammback was dropped, and also the senior Eagle two-door sedan. The SX/4 this year was offered in base, D/L and Sport versions.

For 1983 Eagle four-door sedans were offered in only one trim level, equivalent to a D/L, while the wagon offered that plus Limited and Sport versions. The four-cylinder engine remained standard. A new 2:73 'performance' axle ratio was offered on six-cylinder Eagles with automatic transmissions.

1985 were carried over. The company was making almost no effort to promote the Eagle or keep the brand alive and sales were drifting downward because of that.

Alliance and Encore got new instrument panels, new grilles, and new low profile headlamps. A new Electronic model joined the Encore line,

featuring high-tech digital instrumentation. Alliance got revised tail lamps and added a four-door base model.

The Renault Alpine sports car didn't debut for 1986; its introduction was pushed back to the spring of 1987. Plans to import the Renault Espace minivan were cancelled because the vehicle's cost was too

Renault LeCar for 1983. Before the summer was over AMC announced it was dropping the Renault LeCar from its line-up, along with the 18i sedan. The 18i wagon would continue to be offered.

high. All hopes now rested on Jeep and the new Renault mid-size car that was coming for 1987.

AMC reported another disastrous loss for 1986. For the fiscal year the company's net sales were $3.4 billion, down substantially from the prior year, and the firm lost $91 million. Car sales fell 56 percent to 66,372 and Jeep sales fell eight percent to 221,362.

The big news for 1983 was the introduction of the U.S.-built Renault Alliance, which offered a range of models in base, L, D/L and Limited series. *Motor Trend* magazine named it 'Car of the Year,' the first time an AMC-produced car had been so awarded since 1963.

American Motors didn't bother to issue an annual report for 1986. By the time it was due to appear early in 1987 the reasons for issuing it had become moot. After 34 years AMC had reached the end of the line. Its corporate parent, Renault, was struggling with losses in its own business and was anxious to divest itself of its losing U.S. operations. The whole North American market had proved a bitter experience for the French automaker. Earlier it had bought out VAM, a small company that produced American Motors cars and Jeep vehicles for the Mexican market. Not long after taking over VAM and pouring huge amounts of capital into it the Mexican firm was on the ropes because of upheaval in the Mexican economy.

Renault car production in the U.S. had sunk so low that it had made an agreement to assemble Chrysler products under contract in the Kenosha, Wisconsin plant. Chrysler M-body cars were the first to be built and a follow-up agreement provided for contract assembly of Chrysler's small L-body subcompacts.

At the same time that Renault was looking to sell its ownership in AMC, Chrysler Corporation was looking to acquire other brands. Lee Iacocca, CEO of Chrysler, coveted Jeep. He set in motion the events that led, during the summer of 1987, to AMC's acquisition by Chrysler Corporation in a move dubbed Project Titan.

In regard to its French overlords, AMC had the final laugh. By the time the deal was made to sell out to Chrysler the company had turned the corner. For the first three months of fiscal 1987 sales rose to $1.1 billion and net earnings of $23 million were produced; on an annual basis that would translate to sales of $4.4 billion and profits of $92 million. That is not a completely speculative projection—American Motors acknowledged in a legal proxy statement that it anticipated that second quarter results for 1987 would be about the same as the first quarter. In interviews, management predicted that American Motors would report a full-year profit for 1988.

The final cars from American Motors Corporation were the 1987 models. The Renault Encore was renamed the Alliance hatchback, expanding but not really aiding the line-up of the slow-selling Alliance. A new Renault GTA line was cobbled together by stuffing a 2.0-liter engine into the Alliance body shell, and dressing the whole thing up with body cladding and some detail changes. It was a surprisingly attractive package, offered in two-door sedan and two-door convertible styles, and if it had come two years earlier it probably would have sold in decent numbers. Its chief competitor, VW's GTI, was doing well. Joining the Renault line was a new imported Medallion compact sedan and wagon, though because it was a midyear introduction they were considered 1988

AMC stylists designed a sharp-looking Alliance two-door sedan for the U.S. market. For 1983 the base Alliance two-door offered a starting price of just $5,595, outstanding for a modern, roomy sedan featuring front-wheel drive, fuel injection, an excellent ride and superior handling.

models. The AMC Eagle line carried over again with no significant changes.

The company had revealed at the end of 1985 that it would replace the Eagle in the 1988 calendar year with a 4x4 version of the European Renault R-19 but those plans were tossed in the scrap heap once the Chrysler deal was made. Earlier plans to build a new Eagle on the Alliance platform had already been discarded.

AMC Eagle had only detail changes for 1984. The four-cylinder engine was standard equipment. Fuel economy ratings for the four-cylinder/four-speed combo were 24 mpg in the city and 30 mpg on the highway. The five-speed achieved a rating of 32 mpg for highway driving.

Great looking Eagle wagon for 1984 with optional alloy wheels and outline white letter tires. Note the very functional adjustable roof rack on this car.

The end came for American Motors during the summer of 1987 when the Chrysler deal was consummated. It marked the end of a company that many had predicted wouldn't last beyond 1955, a firm that surprised everyone by outlasting every other American independent automaker.

The deal also marked the end of the Renault brand in the U.S.—whatever Renault cars would still be offered would be marketed under the new Eagle brand name. Chrysler discontinued the AMC name almost immediately and would follow that up by discontinuing the 'true' AMC cars not long after. The final Eagle four-wheel-drive cars were the 1988 models. The line-up was trimmed down to a single station wagon body style and a single model. The 1988 Eagle wagon, base priced at $12,995, now included air conditioning, automatic transmission, and many formerly optional items as standard equipment. But it wasn't meant to last forever. On December 14, 1987, production of the Eagle wagon ceased, ending a proud lineage that stretched back to the dawn of the auto industry.

10 GOOD REASONS WHY EAGLE IS WORTH MORE THAN ANY ORDINARY WAGON.

THE 2-WHEEL/4-WHEEL DRIVE Eagle

With Concord and Spirit gone the only AMC brand cars for 1984 were the Eagles. Eagle prices were $9,495 for the four-door sedan, $10,225 for the regular station wagon, and $10,695 for the Eagle Limited wagon.

AMC's new car for 1984 was the Renault Encore. A variation of the Alliance platform, it was built in the Kenosha, Wisconsin plant.

Renault Alliance D/L for 1984. AMC reported a profit for the year of $15 million—its first since 1979. Wholesale car sales during the fiscal year fell about 28,000 units despite introduction of the new Encore. Jeep sales rose almost 80,000 units and sales of AMC cars and Jeep vehicles rose in international markets.

Alliance L two-door sedan for 1984. During the year AMC announced it had purchased 250 acres of land in Ontario, Canada on which it would construct an automobile assembly plant for production of a new intermediate size car. The new factory would be known as the Bramalea plant.

With sales of its Alliance and Encore beginning to soften in a changing market AMC announced special Diamond Edition models to revive interest in its small cars.

The Eagle line received its final bit of restyling in 1985 when the power-bulge hood design, formerly reserved for SX/4 and Eagle Sport, was adopted for all Eagles.

AMC added a convertible model to the Alliance for 1985; although it was a welcome addition it wasn't enough to revive the struggling Renault line.

The Encore GS for 1985 had a new 1.7-liter engine as standard equipment.

The 1985 Alliance was a good car but had difficulty competing against much better known small cars in a market segment that was rapidly shrinking.

Renault Fuego Turbo for 1985. The French-built Fuego was a fun car to drive but never really caught on with buyers.

The 1986 Eagle Limited station wagon. Again this year Eagle changes or improvements were minimal. The company was making practically no effort to promote the Eagle or keep the brand alive and sales were suffering as a result.

AMC reported another loss for 1986. For the fiscal year the company's net sales were $3.4 billion, down substantially from the prior year, and the firm lost $91 million. Car sales fell 56 percent to 66,372 and Jeep sales fell 8 percent to 221,362.

Renault Alliance and Encore models received new headlamps, a new grille and a new instrument panel for 1986 as sales continued to slide.

The Renault Sportwagon for 1986. As before, these models were imported rather than produced in AMC's plant.

With time running out for AMC, the company introduced the new Renault GTA for 1987. GTA used the Alliance body and a potent 2.0-liter engine. If it had debuted two years earlier it might have sold reasonably well. However, by 1987 few people were interested in buying a Renault-branded product.

Unlike the similar VW GTI, the Renault GTA series offered a conventional two-door sedan, and this convertible too.

During 1987 news broke that Chrysler was buying AMC. Almost completely lost in the confusion was the new Renault Medallion, an imported compact one size up from the Alliance.

To cut marketing costs the Encore was re-badged the Alliance hatchback for 1987. A total of 13 Alliance models were offered that year.

As good as it was, the Alliance only proved the truth of the adage—a car company can't live on only one car. Sales for 1987 were extremely poor.

The performance and dependability of four-wheel drive. A sophisticated, soothing interior. The convenience of cargo space and superb trailering capabilities. Quite simply, Eagle's got it all.

Whether you choose Eagle wagon or sedan, you're making a very intelligent choice. Both come with an impressive list of standard features designed to give you maximum security and comfort. In addition, an extensive list of optional features lets you equip your Eagle to suit your needs.

Through the years, Eagle heritage has grown strong and proud. 1987 is no exception. Eagle truly is a breed apart.

The last time an American Motors brand car would be offered was in 1987, when the AMC Eagle sedan and wagon were marketed by American Motors dealers.

The all-new Premier mid-size car arrived for 1988, too late to change things. This car was produced in the new AMC plant in Canada, and later sold as the Eagle Premier and Dodge Monaco.

Since there no longer was an American Motors, the 1988 Eagle wagon is technically considered an Eagle vehicle, not an AMC. However, in heart and soul it is an AMC—the last car from one of the greatest carmakers of all time.

CHAPTER 8

Looking Back at AMC

It's a shame that AMC is no longer with us. As corporations go, it certainly deserved to continue. AMC served the American driving public's best interests for many years and provided the automotive industry with more innovation than one would ordinarily expect, given its small size. But it was no ordinary company; it was the last, and the very best, of the great independent automakers.

The first production Rambler of 1902 was built by the company that evolved into American Motors. Over the years the firm introduced many innovations including unit body construction in 1941, which virtually every car in the world now uses, the modern heating/ventilating system in 1938, the principles of which are still in use by all car makers, the first seat belts, introduced on the 1950 Nash, the first compact car, the 1950 Rambler, the first American subcompact, the 1970 Gremlin, the first muscle car, the 1957 Rebel; the list goes on and on. America's automotive heritage has been greatly enriched by American Motors.

We missed some great products too. In the late 1970s Styling VP Dick Teague showed sketches of completely restyled Concord/Eagle bodies that were exceptionally attractive. They could have been produced using the existing body, and I'm convinced they would have extended the life span of that evergreen chassis for several more years. Looking at the designs, I also believe they would have sold rather well. It's a pity they weren't put into production. By the mid-1980s the Eagle body looked out of date. Yet buyers loved the Eagle and would have bought many more if only the car could have been given the kind of updated styling that Teague proposed. In addition, AMC had its new 4.0-liter six-cylinder engine that was introduced for 1987. It was a veritable powerhouse and if it had been offered in a restyled Eagle body just imagine how well those cars would have sold. There's the pity—the four-wheel-drive Eagle was too good a car to simply abandon; yet that's just what happened.

I have some official AMC memos in my files that describe what the company called the 'AMC Advanced Four-Wheel-Drive Program,' which would introduce a whole new series of four-wheel-drive cars in several size classes. Apparently the first product was going to be a 4x4 version of the Alliance. If this new product line had come to fruition, built in Kenosha and wearing an AMC Eagle nameplate, who can say how well it might have done? Rather than follow this course Chrysler spent untold millions trying to build name recognition for a new Eagle brand that was aimed at import buyers. Certainly a full line-up of four-wheel-drive Eagles would have been a smarter approach than the direction that Chrysler took. Remember that Subaru took the path of offering only four-wheel-drive vehicles and they are still around. And most certainly, reinvigorating the AMC brand, with its 34-year history and name recognition, would have been a lot smarter than trying to establish a new Eagle brand name. If Chrysler had kept the AMC nameplate it could have spent those millions of dollars on far more productive things, such as new products. It's a shame they didn't.

But is AMC really gone? Judge for yourself. The old American Motors (nee Nash-Kelvinator) headquarters building in Detroit not only still stands; it is still in use as an automotive facility. Men and women report there every working day, heading into the old executive offices and design studios where they work on designing future Jeep and truck models for Chrysler. The more modern AMC headquarters building in Southfield, Michigan that is shown on the cover of the 1980 sales catalog is still called The American Center. Kenosha, Wisconsin is also still very much involved in automotive manufacturing, building engines for Jeep vehicles. Some of these engines are even based on the old AMC six-cylinder. The Bramalea plant that AMC built in Canada is today still building cars– Chrysler brands, however.

AM General, the company world famous for its Hummer line of civilian vehicles and Humvee military trucks is a thriving concern. AM General, you'll recall, was created by AMC. The Hummer was designed by AMC employees. So in a sense there are still AMC vehicles being produced today.

Lastly, there is Jeep. Although many companies have owned Jeep over the years, as of this writing AMC managed it for the longest period of time, and it was AMC management that resurrected Jeep and made it the success it is.

So is AMC really gone? I don't think so. Mediocrity passes away. Imitators are eventually forgotten. But truly great things never really die—they live forever in our memories. They are everlasting.